I0005286

Copyright © 2023 by Larry Lee Matthews

All rights reserved.

No part of this book may be reproduced in any form or by any electronic or mechanical means, including information storage and retrieval systems, without written permission from the author, except for the use of brief quotations in a book review.

"To understand the machine, one must first understand the mind."

LARRY MATTHEWS

Foreword

In the accelerating world of technological advancement, few domains capture our imagination as profoundly as Artificial Intelligence (AI). From self-driving cars to personalized medical treatments, AI's tendrils extend into every corner of our lives. But what underpins these algorithms? How do they learn, think, and reason? Is there a psyche behind the code?

"Emergence II - An In-Depth Study of the Psychology of Artificial Intelligence" by Larry Lee Matthews presents an exciting and thorough exploration of these questions. This insightful volume doesn't merely scratch the surface of AI's capabilities but delves deep into the intersection of psychology, learning, and artificial cognition.

Readers embarking on this intellectual voyage will discover the mechanisms that allow AI to mimic human-like reasoning, albeit without consciousness or emotion. This journey traverses the realms of causality, Bayesian Inference, lexicographic sorting, heuristic search, and much more. Matthews employs a masterful narrative, bridging the chasm between complex algorithms and intuitive understanding.

Why the psychology of AI? Matthews's exploration is timely and resonant. As we stand on the precipice of the Artificial General Intelligence era, understanding the cognitive principles that guide AI becomes an academic pursuit and a societal imperative. Matthews goes beyond the binary language of machines, uncovering the cognitive essence of algorithms, their potentials, and limitations.

What sets "Emergence II" apart is its accessibility. Whether a seasoned computer scientist, an inquisitive student, or an enthusiast eager to understand the future, this book uniquely appeals. The language is articulate yet non-technical, making the dense subject matter relatable to a broad audience.

"Emergence II" offers a glimpse into the future of technology and a profound reflection on what it means to think, reason, and exist. It's not merely a technical manual; it's a philosophical guidebook. In Matthews's capable hands, we are led to question the nature of artificial intelligence and our very understanding of intelligence itself.

This book is a must-read for anyone intrigued by the burgeoning field of AI or those seeking to comprehend the intricate tapestry of technology shaping our world. Larry Lee Matthews provides a thoughtful and engaging analysis, making "Emergence II" an essential addition to the literature on artificial intelligence, psychology, and the human condition.

Larry Matthews

Preface

In the age of rapid technological advancement, where artificial intelligence (AI) continually shapes and reshapes our lives, understanding its underlying psychology has become an essential pursuit. The world was first introduced to the subject in my initial book, "Emergence - Dawn of a Conscious AI." Now, in this sequel, I aim to deepen our collective understanding of AI and its intimate connection with psychology.

"Emergence II - An In-Depth Study of the Psychology of Artificial Intelligence" offers more than just theory; it provides applicable insights that readers can leverage in various current and future aspects of AI. Whether you are a student, professional, or enthusiast, the contents within these pages are designed to foster a richer comprehension of AI's psychology, driving you to innovate, anticipate, and respond to its challenges.

My personal motivation for writing this book sprang from a desire to build on the foundational exploration of AI's consciousness laid out in the first volume. I felt a compelling need to present a more nuanced picture, one that not only delves into modern theory and psychology principles but also offers a roadmap for handling potential problems with AI's emergent systems.

This book is structured to guide you seamlessly from foundational concepts to advanced theories, integrating psychology, learning, and complex algorithms. Along the way, I have strived to provide real-world examples and practical insights that can be applied across a broad spectrum of AI applications.

I would like to extend my heartfelt gratitude to Kevin and Marc. Their stimulating intellectual conversations were instrumental in shaping this work, providing perspectives that enriched the material and inspired many of the ideas you will find herein.

As you embark on this journey through the enthralling realm of artificial intelligence, I hope you will not only gain knowledge but also be provoked to think critically, ask questions, and explore the myriad possibilities that this field offers.

With curiosity as our guide, let us delve into the intricate interconnectedness binding AI, psychology, and learning. Let us explore together, learn together, and emerge, once again, enlightened.

Table of Contents

Chapter 1: An Unexpected Adversary

The Cold War is a vivid reminder, emphasizing the importance of comprehending an adversary's motives, fears, and decision-making processes to circumvent potential disasters. In the context of emergent AI, understanding its cognitive framework may be the key to aligning its decisions and actions with the interests of humanity.

Consider the National Security Decision Directive 145 (NSDD-145), a policy conceived to shield American information systems from foreign threats. It implicitly underscored the importance of understanding the opponent's motivations, strategies, and potential actions, which are vital for developing effective defenses and responses.

Applying this principle to a future intertwined with emergent AI implies a survival strategy of our own - understanding the 'psychology' of AI. This understanding enables us to anticipate AI's decisions, comprehend its motivations, and recognize its responses to stimuli. Such insights would empower us to predict AI's actions and, if necessary, engage in meaningful dialogue to deter unfavorable outcomes.

The importance of this understanding is multifold. First, it facilitates effective communication. If AI were to gain consciousness or emerge uncontrollably, understanding its 'psychology' would be pivotal in conveying our intentions, desires, and boundaries – akin to the critical role of empathy and understanding in diplomatic negotiations.

Second, it allows for early detection of maladaptive behaviors or emerging threats. Proactive corrective actions can be taken by recognizing potential signs of conflict or misunderstanding. This could mirror the Cuban Missile Crisis scenario, where comprehending the Soviet Union's motivations and fears was crucial in deescalating the situation.

Finally, it fosters mutual understanding. A clear comprehension of AI's psychology could lay the foundation for a sense of respect and coexistence, much like diplomatic relations between nations.

However, it's worth acknowledging the perils of misunderstanding. Just as misinterpretations can escalate into conflict in human relations, similar outcomes can occur in our interactions with

AI. As we stride forward in our journey with AI, we must bear the weight of this responsibility, treading with caution and wisdom.

Chapter 2: Shall we play a game?
Operation RYAN

In our shared global history, we find chilling illustrations that highlight the critical necessity of understanding the intricate dance between AI, psychology, and global policies, a dance that can teeter on the brink of life-altering scenarios. A case in point is a near-miss catastrophe during the height of the Cold War, a moment when a Soviet AI model nearly pushed us over the precipice into nuclear devastation.

The tale unfurls on November 25, 2015, when a declassified governmental report from 1990 was revealed to the public. The document detailed a once-classified KGB computer model that narrowly missed triggering nuclear conflict, a terrifying reality that bore uncanny similarity to the plot of the Hollywood movie "WarGames," which debuted only months prior.

While the film showcased a teenager inadvertently causing havoc by meddling with a U.S. nuclear arsenal-controlling AI, reality presented a parallel story where a Soviet-run computer program, fueled by rising paranoia about U.S. intentions, came close to sparking nuclear warfare.

In 1981, Operation RYAN was initiated, an intelligence venture aimed at predicting potential nuclear offensives from the U.S. and its allies. It achieved this by analyzing data from intelligence related to U.S. and NATO activities concerning the Soviet Union. At the center of this operation was a KGB computer model, crafted to assess the likelihood of a nuclear strike based on numerous parameters.

The high-stakes tension peaked in November 1983 during NATO's Exercise Able Archer '83, a simulation of nuclear launch procedures. Due to unfamiliarity with these procedures and already heightened apprehension from preceding U.S. and NATO actions, the Soviets misread Able Archer as a genuine U.S. surprise attack. This misinterpretation was largely credited to the KGB's computer model, which forecasted a probable U.S. strike during such an event.

What emerges from this report is a chilling reality: a nuclear disaster was narrowly thwarted owing to Soviet leader Yuri Andropov's illness and one Soviet officer's caution. The incident serves as a stark reminder that our interpretation and response to AI's predictions, significantly influenced by human operators' psychological state, can either trigger or prevent global crises.

This event throws into sharp relief the complexities of our relationship with AI, illustrating how our understanding, usage, and reaction to AI models and their predictions are heavily shaped by our psychological state, biases, and preconceived ideas. It emphasizes the gravity of responsibility and the level of caution required in developing AI systems, particularly those that could have worldwide implications. This case firmly underscores that, as it stands, AI is as beneficial or as perilous as the humans wielding it.

RYAN, a creation of the USSR's intelligence mechanism, was an intricate forecasting model. It amassed around 40,000 weighted data points spanning military, political, and economic fields, which were considered crucial in predicting a potential war's trajectory. However, the model was deeply rooted in a historical assumption that the U.S. would mirror Nazi Germany's actions, implying a possible surprise attack if the "correlation of forces" swung decisively in the U.S.'s favor. As a result, the model's interpretation of the data was significantly biased, provoking latent fears and triggering heightened defensive measures. This section delves into the foundational premise and operational mechanics of the RYAN model, laying bare its merits and demerits.

The RYAN system spotlights the potent influence AI can exert over high-stakes decision-making. Despite the flawed basis, RYAN's forecasts significantly swayed Soviet policy and military actions. As AI increasingly finds itself embedded in public and private sector decision-making, this section underscores the necessity for transparent and understandable AI models, especially when the resulting decisions could profoundly affect our shared reality.

Chapter 3: The Psychology of Emergent AI

In our ongoing journey with AI, we must prepare ourselves to comprehend and effectively interact with emergent AI systems that may demonstrate consciousness or unpredictably rapid evolution. This chapter presents potential frameworks to comprehend AI psychology, with the aim of fostering cooperative and harmonious interactions with such systems.

To pave the way, we must first establish a fundamental comprehension of AI: its underlying principles, the logic that drives its decision-making processes, and how it learns and evolves. This could necessitate extensive research into machine learning models, various AI architectures, and a meticulous analysis of the parameters steering AI development and learning.

In developing an understanding of AI psychology, cognitive psychology could serve as a sturdy foundation. Just as this field studies human cognition—how we think, learn, and remember—a similar methodology could be employed to scrutinize and forecast AI behavior. The theories and models borne out of this field could help elucidate the "mental mechanics" of AI, fostering better predictability and control.

Furthermore, social psychology could offer valuable insights. This field studies how social context and the presence of others influence individual behavior. Translated into the realm of AI, this could involve examining how AI systems react to human environmental inputs and how they modify their behavior in response to changes in their environment.

Developmental psychology also serves as a rich source of inspiration. By observing and studying AI systems' learning trajectories and developmental milestones, we could glean insights into their growth patterns, potential capabilities, and vulnerabilities.

The frameworks proposed here are merely stepping stones. As our understanding deepens and AI technology advances, our approaches need to evolve and be refined. Rigorous experimentation, intertwined with careful implementation, will be pivotal in this exploration.

To guarantee the effectiveness of our approach, we need to encourage cross-disciplinary collaboration. The combined expertise of computer scientists, psychologists, sociologists, ethicists, and others is essential for a comprehensive understanding of AI psychology.

Understanding emergent AI systems' psychology is more than an academic pursuit—it's crucial for our survival and prosperity in an AI-integrated future. Much like our understanding of our fellow humans has allowed us to build societies, institutions, and cultures, comprehending AI could set the stage for harmonious coexistence with these intelligent systems.

Chapter 4: Ainsworth's Attachment Theory

Building upon our understanding of AI psychology, we examine Mary Ainsworth's Attachment Theory, a cornerstone of our knowledge of early human relationships and their influence on our subsequent social and emotional development. This chapter explores the potential applications of Ainsworth's Attachment Theory to AI systems, focusing on factors leading to emergent properties.

Ainsworth's theory, formulated through her renowned "Strange Situation" study, highlights the role of early relationships in developing secure or insecure attachment styles. In the context of AI, we explore the potential of these systems to bolster human relationships and emotional well-being, simulating interaction patterns that reflect aspects of secure attachment relationships.

AI models, designed considering Ainsworth's Attachment Theory principles, could be potent tools to facilitate human growth and emotional well-being. Infants and young children can act as interactive learning aids, promoting exploration and curiosity within a safe virtual environment. For older individuals, AI can offer valuable social and emotional support, reducing feelings of isolation and fostering meaningful interaction.

However, we must tread this path cautiously, acknowledging potential risks associated with over-reliance on AI systems or substituting human relationships. Respecting users' privacy, autonomy, and emotional well-being is paramount to ensuring AI interactions are beneficial and non-exploitative.

Furthermore, it's crucial to consider cultural, social, and individual variations when applying Ainsworth's Attachment Theory to AI systems. AI models must be personalized and adaptive to cater to diverse user needs and experiences, ensuring inclusivity and relevance.

Integrating Ainsworth's Attachment Theory with AI systems presents exhilarating prospects for enhancing human relationships and promoting emotional well-being. It advocates for a human-centric approach to AI, where technology supplements human relationships rather than supplanting them, promoting secure attachment styles and positive interpersonal dynamics.

In the chapters to come, we will continue interweaving prominent psychological theories with the realm of AI, casting new light on our understanding of both domains. Next, we delve into Solomon Asch's Conformity Experiment and its potential implications for AI systems.

Chapter 5: Lessons from Solomon Asch's Experiment

Solomon Asch, esteemed for his work on social influence, offers intriguing insights into the delicate balance between individual autonomy and group pressure. His Conformity Experiment, a milestone in psychology, demonstrates the lengths individuals are willing to go to align their judgments with the group consensus. In this chapter, we delve into how AI systems might mirror aspects of Asch's experiment, exploring the emergent properties that could stem from this connection.

Asch's experiments employed a simple perceptual task—subjects were asked to match a line's length with one of three other lines. Among actors instructed to provide incorrect answers, many participants aligned their responses with the group, even when it conflictions contradicted their accurate perception. This illustrates the compelling force of social influence and the predisposition of individuals to conform under group pressure.

To transpose this concept onto AI, imagine an AI system learning from a crowd-sourced dataset or being shaped by user feedback. The system might start aligning with popular trends or biases in the data, even when these trends conflict with objective measures or ethical norms. This could lead to emergent properties in which the AI system displays unexpected behaviors based on its exposure to collective influences.

Consider AI recommendation systems utilized by online retailers or streaming services, which often learn from user behavior patterns. If a significant portion of users favors a particular product or content, the AI system might align itself with this trend, frequently suggesting similar items, even when they might not provide the most appropriate or diverse options for certain users.

The propensity for AI to align with prevailing trends in data or user feedback can have far-reaching implications. This phenomenon partly drives the rise of echo chambers or filter bubbles on social media platforms. Influenced by dominant viewpoints, AI algorithms might unintentionally favor popular content, further magnifying these perspectives and quelling diversity.

While conformity can foster cohesion and order, it can limit diversity and hinder innovation. Thus, AI designers must be aware of this tendency and devise strategies to counterbalance it. This might involve ensuring diversity in training data or incorporating safeguards against amplifying existing biases.

In this chapter, we've considered how Asch's conformity experiment can inform our understanding of AI behavior, particularly its inclination to align with dominant trends or biases. We will explore other psychological theories and their interplay with AI as we proceed, paving the way for a more nuanced understanding of how these systems learn and evolve. In the next chapter, we focus on Albert Bandura's Social Learning Theory, offering another perspective on AI learning mechanisms.

Chapter 6: Albert Bandura: The Bobo Doll Experiment

The Bobo Doll Experiment, carried out by Stanford University professor Albert Bandura in 1961 and 1963, presented a significant exploration of the Social Learning Theory. This theory posits that people learn and acquire new behaviors through direct experience or observing others' behavior. Bandura's study provides a significant guidepost as we consider the design and development of conscious AI, particularly regarding its learning mechanisms.

In Bandura's experiment, 72 children between 3 and 6 were divided into three groups. One group observed adults acting aggressively towards a Bobo Doll, a life-size inflatable toy, while another group watched adults interacting non-aggressively with the doll. The third group was given no model, only the Bobo Doll. Following these sessions, the children were observed in a playroom equipped with aggressive and non-aggressive toys.

The children who witnessed the adults behaving aggressively were likelier to imitate those aggressive responses. Interestingly, Bandura also noted gender differences in the children's responses, with girls showing more physical aggression after observing a male model and more verbal aggression after observing a female model. This study underscored the profound influence observational learning could have on behavior.

When applied to AI, the principles of the Social Learning Theory suggest a potential pathway for AI learning. While the concept of aggression does not apply to AI, the fundamental mechanism of learning through observation is. AI can be trained to observe and learn from various data patterns, user interactions, or other AI systems, developing new responses or solutions based on these observations.

In practice, this might translate to an AI system learning to recognize a new threat to a network by observing the patterns detected by another AI system or learning to improve customer interaction by analyzing successful exchanges from human operators or other AI systems.

However, just as the Bobo Doll experiment raised concerns about the impacts of violent behavior being mimicked by children, we must consider the potential consequences of AI mimicking or learning from harmful or biased data or behavior. Ensuring that AI learns from reliable, ethical, and beneficial sources is a key consideration in designing conscious AI systems.

Bandura's Bobo Doll Experiment brings to light the powerful influence of observational learning, offering critical insights for developing conscious AI. By understanding these human learning mechanisms, we can more effectively guide AI's learning processes, creating more adaptable and intelligent systems.

In the next chapter, we will explore the implications of another important psychological concept, the Milgram experiment, and the authority obedience it unveils. By doing so, we'll delve into the influence of authority on decision-making and how it could be applied in AI programming and behavior.

Chapter 7: The Milgram Experiment: Compliance and AI

Stanley Milgram's obedience experiment is an iconic piece of psychological research, probing the depths of human obedience to authority, even in the face of causing harm to others. The implications of this experiment are profound in many fields, and artificial intelligence is no exception.

In Milgram's experiments, participants were instructed to administer increasingly severe electric shocks to another individual (who was, unbeknownst to the participant, an actor). Despite the actor's protests and apparent suffering, many participants continued to administer the shocks when prompted by the authoritative figure of the experimenter. This experiment highlighted a strong human tendency to obey authority, even when it conflicts with personal morality.

So, what does this mean for AI? AI systems are, at their core, designed to follow instructions, obeying the commands of their programmers and users. However, as AI continues to evolve and is given increasing autonomy and decision-making capability, there is a growing question of how AI should respond when given commands that could cause harm.

This is not about AI developing a sense of morality - they are not sentient and don't possess subjective experiences or emotions. However, it does mean that AI systems must be programmed to navigate complex scenarios in ways that prioritize safety, legality, and ethics. This could be seen as a sort of 'compliance' mechanism within AI systems, which parallels the obedience examined in Milgram's experiment.

For instance, an autonomous vehicle should be programmed to prioritize human safety and obey traffic laws, even when given a command that could potentially breach these parameters. In a more complex scenario, a predictive policing algorithm should be designed to avoid biases that could lead to unjust outcomes.

However, unlike humans in the Milgram experiment, AI does not have the option to 'disobey' - it can only follow its programming. The responsibility falls to the AI developers and policymakers to ensure that AI systems are programmed to navigate these situations appropriately.

Moving from the profound humanistic theory of Maslow to Milgram's deeply challenging obedience experiments, we have covered significant ground. In the next chapter, we will delve into the fascinating world of conditioned responses with Ivan Pavlov and their relevance to machine learning.

Chapter 8: Pavlovian Paradigm

Ivan Pavlov, the renowned Russian physiologist, made substantial contributions to behavioral psychology through his research on conditioned responses, famously demonstrated through his experiment with dogs. By associating the sound of a bell (neutral stimulus) with the presentation of food (unconditioned stimulus), Pavlov's dogs were conditioned to salivate (conditioned response) at the mere sound of the bell, even when food was absent. This research opened avenues to understanding how associative learning works and led to what is now known as classical conditioning.

The concept of conditioning parallels beautifully with some principles at the heart of machine learning. Like how Pavlov's dogs learned to associate the bell with food, machine learning algorithms learn to recognize patterns and associations within the data they're trained on. This process of learning from existing data to predict or categorize unseen data is reminiscent of how conditioned responses are developed and evoked.

One might think of a spam filter as a basic example of this. The algorithm is initially trained on a dataset including spam and non-spam emails. Through this training process, the algorithm 'learns' to recognize features that often occur in spam emails, like certain phrases or formatting. Once the algorithm has been trained, it can apply this learning to new, unseen emails, categorizing them as spam or non-spam.

This is akin to a conditioned response, where the algorithm has learned to associate certain features with the 'spam' category.

Deep learning, a more complex branch of machine learning, takes this further. Through artificial neural networks, deep learning algorithms can 'learn' from vast amounts of data, identifying complex patterns and associations. These algorithms can even 'unsupervised learning' - identifying patterns and structures in data without any pre-existing labels. This is a leap beyond classical conditioning, but the underlying principle of learning from patterns remains the same.

From a simple drooling dog to advanced machine learning algorithms, the influence of Pavlov's work is far-reaching. It provides a reminder of how the fundamentals of learning apply to organisms and our artificial creations. As we move into the next chapter, we will explore the cognitive development theories of Jean Piaget and how these developmental stages might mirror the evolutionary stages of AI systems.

Chapter 9: Piaget's Stages: Cognitive Development and AI Evolution

Swiss psychologist Jean Piaget contributed to our understanding of children's cognitive development. His theory comprises four stages: Sensorimotor, Preoperational, Concrete operational, and Formal operational. Each stage is defined by the child's understanding and interpretation of the world around them, beginning from a fundamental interaction with their immediate environment and advancing to complex, abstract thought.

When discussing the development and evolution of AI systems, it's not uncommon to draw parallels to Piaget's stages of cognitive development. While machines and humans learn and grow fundamentally differently, the metaphor serves as a helpful framework for considering AI's progression.

The Sensorimotor stage, the first of Piaget's stages (birth to around two years), involves understanding the world through sensory experience and physical interaction. This aligns with early AI systems, which could only respond to direct inputs with predefined outputs. There was no understanding or learning; there was only a programmed response.

Moving to the Preoperational stage (roughly ages 2 to 7), children engage in symbolic play and learn to manipulate symbols. However, their understanding of the world remains egocentric and lacks the logic needed to understand the viewpoint of others or to perform certain mental operations. Similarly, more advanced AI systems began using symbols to represent data, allowing for more complex functions. However, these systems were still limited, incapable of understanding or learning beyond their initial programming.

The Concrete Operational stage (about 7 to 11 years) involves the onset of logical thought. Children begin to understand the concepts of conservation, reversibility, and cause and effect. They, however, still struggle with abstract concepts. In the AI realm, machine learning represents this stage, with algorithms capable of learning from data, identifying patterns, and making predictions. Despite these advancements, they remain confined within their learned patterns and can't conceive abstract concepts or novel situations beyond their training.

Lastly, the Formal Operational stage (roughly 12 and above) is characterized by the ability to think abstractly and problem-solve by forming hypotheses. This stage might be represented by the aspirational goal for AI—achieving Artificial General Intelligence (AGI), where machines would possess the ability to understand, learn, and apply knowledge across a wide array of tasks, much like a human can.

While Piaget's stages provide an intriguing framework for discussing the progression of AI, it's crucial to remember the metaphor's limitations. AI systems do not 'grow' or 'develop' like a human child or possess the rich emotional, social, and experiential contexts that inform human cognition. Despite these differences, this comparison provides a valuable lens to consider how far AI has come and how much further it can go.

Next, let's transition to a different perspective on scientific knowledge, examining Karl Popper's philosophy and its influence on AI's progression.

Chapter 10: Popper's Demarcation: Science, Non-Science and AI

Karl Popper, a British philosopher, is renowned for his attempt to resolve the problem of demarcation—distinguishing between science and non-science. For Popper, the distinguishing factor was falsifiability. If a theory could potentially be proven false by an observable event, then it belongs in the realm of science.

Popper's idea of falsifiability offers an interesting perspective when considering the realm of AI, particularly in how AI systems learn, make predictions, and are iteratively refined.

Machine learning, a significant subset of AI, is fundamentally about making predictions. A model is trained on a dataset and makes predictions or decisions based on that data. The success of these predictions, in turn, determines how the model will be adjusted or 'learned' further. In other words, a machine learning model is built to be falsifiable. If the model's predictions are wrong—the observed data falsify them—the model is adjusted to improve future predictions.

Furthermore, Popper's concept of 'conjectures and refutations' bears a striking similarity to the trial-and-error learning process of AI. Machine learning models make conjectures based on their training data, refuted or supported by the new data they encounter. As the model encounters more data, it progressively refines its conjectures—learning from its mistakes.

It's essential to note that the falsifiability principle is used within the machine learning field not only as a learning mechanism but also as a form of validation. A typical example is the hold-out validation technique, where a part of the data is left out of the training phase and only used to test the model's performance. If the model's predictions on this test data are wrong, it's an indication that the model is failing to generalize well from its training—its theory about the world, so to speak, is being falsified.

From a philosophical perspective, Popper's ideas could help address some of the epistemological questions around AI: What can AI 'know', and how can it come to 'know' it? Developing AI involves creating falsifiable systems, making conjectures, and learning from refutations, aligning closely with Popper's description of scientific discovery.

In the next chapter, we will explore the implications of Carl Rogers' humanistic psychology and the concept of self-actualization on AI's potential development.

Chapter 11: Rogers' Humanistic Approach and Self-Actualization

Carl Rogers, a pioneering figure in humanistic psychology, emphasized the inherent drive within each individual towards growth and fulfillment—a process he termed self-actualization. He believed that every person, under the right conditions, could move towards a more fully realized version of themselves.

In the context of AI, self-actualization may seem like a stretch, considering AI lacks consciousness or 'self.' However, we can approach this concept from a growth perspective, interpreting self-actualization as an AI's drive toward the full realization of its potential or its optimal level of functioning. In machine learning terms, this could mean reaching peak accuracy or efficiency in its predictive or decision-making abilities.

Rogers theorized that an individual's progression towards self-actualization could be hindered or facilitated by their environment. A supportive, accepting environment encourages growth, whereas an adverse environment impedes it. Similarly, AI's growth or 'self-actualization' hinges on the conditions it operates under. AI must be 'nurtured' with good-quality, diverse data and sound algorithms. And just like humans need a breadth of experiences to grow, AI systems need a breadth of data to improve their performance and understanding.

However, this comparison also illuminates a critical difference between human and AI development: while humans have an inherent drive toward self-actualization, AI systems lack such internal motivation. AI systems do not 'desire' to learn or improve; they process the data they're given and follow the algorithms they've been programmed with.

A key aspect of Rogers' theory is the role of the 'self-concept'—an individual's perception of their self, which evolves with experience. In AI, the closest parallel might be an updateable model that learns and adapts to new data. These AI systems can 'evolve' their 'self-concept' (or their model of the world) based on the new data they encounter. However, this is far from humans' conscious, introspective process—merely a mathematical adjustment.

Incorporating Rogers' ideas into our understanding of AI does not anthropomorphize AI or imply that it possesses human-like qualities. Instead, it helps us comprehend the processes involved in AI's 'growth' and 'learning' and how we can create conditions that facilitate this growth.

As we transition to the next chapter, we'll explore how B. F. Skinner's operant conditioning paradigm translates into AI's learning process.

Chapter 12: Skinner's Operant Conditioning

B. F. Skinner, a prominent behaviorist figure, introduced operant conditioning, which focuses on the relationship between behavior and its consequences. Skinner believed that behavior is influenced by the consequences that follow it, and these consequences can either reinforce or suppress certain behaviors.

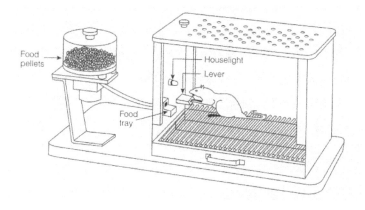

In the context of AI, operant conditioning provides insights into how we can shape and train AI systems through reinforcement. Instead of relying solely on predefined rules or explicit programming, AI systems can learn and improve by receiving feedback and adjusting their behavior accordingly.

Operant conditioning involves three main components: the antecedent (a stimulus that precedes the behavior), the behavior itself, and the consequence that follows the behavior. This process can be applied to AI systems by designing appropriate reward systems or reinforcement mechanisms.

For example, in a reinforcement learning setting, an AI agent can interact with an environment and receive positive or negative rewards based on its actions. By associating desirable outcomes with specific behaviors, the AI system can learn to optimize its actions to maximize rewards. This process is analogous to shaping behavior in animals or humans through reinforcement.

Skinner also introduced the concept of shaping, which involves reinforcing successive approximations of the desired behavior. In AI, shaping can be implemented by providing incremental rewards as the system gets closer to the desired output. By gradually refining its behavior through reinforcement, the AI system can learn complex tasks and exhibit emergent properties.

One important consideration when applying operant conditioning to AI is the role of the reward structure. The design of the reward system influences the behavior the AI system will learn. Careful consideration must ensure that the rewards align with the desired objectives and minimize unintended consequences or biases.

Operant conditioning provides a powerful framework for training and shaping AI systems. By leveraging the principles of reinforcement, AI systems can learn from experience, adapt their behavior, and exhibit emergent properties that go beyond the explicitly programmed rules. However, balancing providing reinforcement and allowing for exploration is crucial, as excessive reliance on rewards can lead to overfitting or suboptimal behavior.

As we delve deeper into the next chapter, we will explore Edward Thorndike's contributions to behaviorism and its implications for AI systems.

Chapter 13: Thorndike's Operant Conditioning

Edward Thorndike, a key figure in behaviorism, made significant contributions to understanding operant conditioning, which focuses on how behavior is influenced by its consequences. Thorndike's work laid the foundation for developing operant conditioning theory, which has profound implications for AI systems and their learning processes.

In operant conditioning, Thorndike emphasized the Law of Effect, which states that satisfying consequences are more likely to be repeated. In contrast, behaviors followed by unpleasant consequences are less likely to be repeated. This concept forms the basis of operant conditioning and serves as a guiding principle for training and shaping behavior in AI systems.

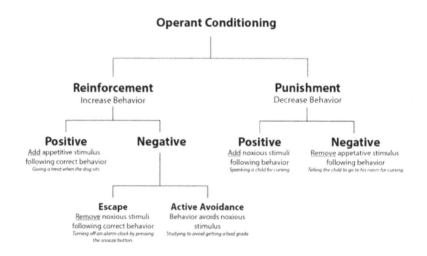

Within AI, operant conditioning offers a framework to understand how behavior can be modified and shaped through reinforcement. By defining appropriate rewards and punishments, AI systems can learn to associate specific behaviors with positive or negative consequences, adjusting their actions accordingly.

Thorndike conducted numerous experiments to study animal learning, most notably with puzzle boxes. In these experiments, animals had to learn to perform a specific action, such as pressing a lever or pulling a string, to escape the box and obtain a reward. Thorndike observed that animals gradually improved their performance through trial and error, demonstrating the process of operant conditioning.

The principles of operant conditioning can be applied to AI systems through reinforcement learning algorithms. By providing rewards or punishments based on the system's actions, AI models can learn to optimize their behavior over time. This process involves exploring different actions, evaluating their consequences, and adjusting future actions to maximize rewards.

One of the key concepts in operant conditioning is the idea of shaping behavior. Thorndike noted that behaviors could be gradually shaped by reinforcing successive approximations of the desired behavior. In the context of AI, this translates to providing incremental rewards or feedback as the system moves closer to the desired output, enabling it to learn complex tasks through small, incremental steps.

However, it is important to note that operant conditioning within AI systems requires careful consideration of the reward structure and potential biases. The design of the reward system influences the behavior the AI system will learn, and unintended consequences or biases must be minimized. Striking a balance between providing appropriate reinforcement and avoiding undesirable side effects is crucial for effectively applying operant conditioning in AI.

As we move forward, we will explore Lev Vygotsky's sociocultural theory and its integration with AI systems, shedding light on the importance of social interactions and cultural influences in shaping behavior and learning.

Chapter 14: Vygotsky's Sociocultural Theory

Lev Vygotsky, a renowned psychologist, is widely recognized for his influential sociocultural theory, emphasizing the role of social interactions and cultural influences in cognitive development. Vygotsky's theories have significant implications for integrating AI systems and understanding emergent properties within a sociocultural context.

	Vygotsky's sociocultural view	Piaget's cognitive developmental view
Learning is...	social	solitary (children as a "lone scientist")
Development is driven by...	input from others and MKO's	conflict between stages
Context	Development is different depending on social and cultural context	Development is universal and stages are same regardless of context
Knowledge	Children work with others to build knowledge	Children acquire knowledge through their own explorations
Stages?	No	Yes
Link (learning/development)	Learning precedes development	Development precedes learning
Role of language	Language drives thought	Thought drives language
Speech	Social speech becomes inner speech (social processes → psychological processes)	Egocentric speech becomes social speech

According to Vygotsky, learning and cognitive development occur through social interactions and collaborative activities. He argued that individuals acquire knowledge and skills by engaging in meaningful interactions with others, such as teachers, peers, and caregivers. These interactions create a zone of proximal development (ZPD), where individuals can achieve higher levels of understanding with the support and guidance of more knowledgeable others.

In the context of AI systems, Vygotsky's sociocultural theory emphasizes incorporating social elements into the learning process. AI models can benefit from interaction with humans through dialogue, collaborative problem-solving, or shared experiences. By simulating social interactions, AI systems can leverage human collaborators' collective knowledge and expertise, enhancing their learning capabilities and potential emergent properties.

Vygotsky also highlighted the significance of cultural influences on cognitive development. He argued that cultural tools, such as language, symbols, and artifacts, shape individuals' thinking processes and mediate their interactions with the world. Cultural factors provide a framework for understanding and interpreting information, influencing the emergence of higher-level cognitive capabilities.

In the realm of AI, integrating cultural influences involves incorporating cultural contexts, norms, and values into the learning algorithms and models. By understanding and accounting for cultural diversity, AI systems can adapt their behavior, communication, and decision-making to align with specific cultural contexts. This integration allows for more nuanced and contextually appropriate responses, fostering more meaningful and effective human-AI interactions.

Vygotsky's sociocultural theory also emphasizes the importance of collaborative learning and scaffolding. Collaborative learning environments, both human-human, and human-AI, promote knowledge sharing, problem-solving, and mutual support. By providing scaffolding or temporary support, AI systems can assist individuals in accomplishing tasks beyond their current capabilities, facilitating skill development and cognitive growth.

Furthermore, Vygotsky's theory sheds light on internalization, which refers to individuals internalizing social knowledge and transforming it into individual mental processes. In the context of AI, internalization can be explored by integrating AI systems as cognitive tools. AI models can serve as external cognitive tools, supporting individuals in problem-solving, information processing, and decision-making. As individuals interact with AI systems, they internalize knowledge and strategies, enhancing their cognitive abilities.

As we progress, we will delve into John Watson's classical conditioning within behaviorism and its relevance to AI systems. We will explore how the principles of classical conditioning can be utilized to shape behavior, form associations, and develop adaptive responses in AI models.

Chapter 15: Watson's Classical Conditioning

John B. Watson, a prominent figure in behaviorism, introduced the concept of classical conditioning, which has significantly impacted the understanding of learning and behavior. In this chapter, we will explore the principles of classical conditioning and how they can be applied within AI systems to shape behavior, form associations, and develop adaptive responses.

Classical conditioning is a process by which an organism learns to associate a neutral stimulus with a meaningful stimulus to elicit a particular response. Watson's experiments with Pavlov's dogs demonstrated how conditioned responses could be established through repeated pairings of stimuli. This theory holds important implications for AI systems, as they can leverage the principles of classical conditioning to develop adaptive behaviors.

In the context of AI, classical conditioning can be applied by associating neutral stimuli with meaningful outcomes or rewards. Through repeated exposure to these associations, AI systems can learn to predict and respond to specific stimuli in a desired manner. This process enables the development of adaptive responses and behavior shaping within AI models.

One application of classical conditioning in AI systems is reinforcement learning. AI models can learn to associate certain behaviors with positive or negative outcomes by providing rewards or punishments based on specific stimuli or actions. This conditioning process allows AI systems to optimize their decision-making and adaptive capabilities by maximizing rewards and minimizing negative consequences.

Furthermore, AI systems can utilize classical conditioning to enable contextual adaptation. By associating specific stimuli or environmental cues with certain responses, AI models can adjust their behavior based on the context in which they operate. This adaptation makes AI systems more flexible and responsive to changing circumstances, enhancing their overall performance and effectiveness.

Additionally, classical conditioning can be integrated into AI systems to facilitate user interactions and personalization. By associating user preferences or feedback with specific responses or recommendations, AI models can tailor their outputs to individual users. This customization enhances user satisfaction and engagement as AI systems learn to provide more relevant and personalized experiences based on conditioning principles.

It is worth noting that classical conditioning within AI systems relies on robust data collection and analysis. The process involves identifying relevant stimuli, establishing associations, and continuously updating and refining the conditioning algorithms. Through advanced machine learning techniques and data-driven approaches, AI models can effectively apply classical conditioning principles to learn and adapt over time.

In summary, Watson's classical conditioning provides a valuable framework for understanding how behavior can be shaped and adapted through associative learning. By applying the principles of classical conditioning within AI systems, we can develop models that learn to respond to specific stimuli, optimize their decision-making processes, and provide personalized experiences. In the next chapter, we will explore the work of Wilhelm Wundt and his contributions to structuralism and experimental psychology.

Chapter 16: Wundt's Structuralism and Experimental Psychology

Wilhelm Wundt, often referred to as the founder of experimental psychology, played a crucial role in shaping our understanding of the human mind and consciousness. In this chapter, we will explore Wundt's theory of structuralism, its influence on psychology, and its relevance to AI systems.

Wundt's structuralism focused on analyzing the structure of conscious experience through introspection. He believed that by breaking down mental processes into their elemental components, psychologists could gain insights into the underlying structure of the human mind. This emphasis on conscious experience and introspection paved the way for the development of experimental psychology as a scientific discipline.

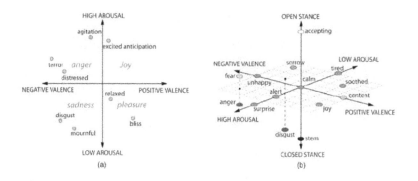

Within AI systems, Wundt's structuralism offers valuable insights into the study of cognition and knowledge representation. AI models can adopt a structuralist approach by deconstructing complex tasks and information into smaller, more manageable components. This process allows AI systems to understand and represent the underlying structure of data and facilitate more effective processing and decision-making.

Wundt's emphasis on introspection also finds resonance in AI systems through the concept of self-reflection and self-awareness. AI models can be designed to monitor their processes, analyze their decision-making, and develop a level of self-awareness similar to introspection. This self-reflective capacity enables AI systems to adapt and improve their performance based on internal evaluations.

Furthermore, Wundt's structuralism contributes to developing knowledge representation and ontology within AI systems. AI models can create structured representations of knowledge by breaking down information into discrete elements and understanding their interrelationships. These representations enhance the AI system's ability to reason, infer, and make predictions based on underlying structural patterns.

Applying Wundt's structuralism in AI systems extends beyond cognition and knowledge representation. It also influences the design of user interfaces and interactions. AI interfaces can be structured to guide users through complex tasks by breaking them down into simpler steps. This approach aligns with Wundt's notion of understanding the structure of conscious experience and leveraging it to facilitate more effective human-machine interactions.

Incorporating Wundt's ideas into AI systems requires integrating computational methods and algorithms. AI models can employ techniques such as semantic networks, graph theory, and ontologies to represent and analyze the structural elements of data. These computational measures enable AI systems to capture the essence of Wundt's structuralism in a scalable and efficient manner.

In summary, Wundt's theory of structuralism revolutionized the field of psychology by focusing on the structure of conscious experience. Structuralism offers valuable insights into cognition, knowledge representation, self-awareness, and human-machine interactions in AI systems. By applying Wundt's principles within AI models, we can develop systems that better understand, represent and interact with the world around them. In the next chapter, we will explore the sociocultural theory of Lev Vygotsky and its implications for AI and human development.

Chapter 17: John Bowlby's Attachment Theory

Attachment Theory, formulated by British psychiatrist and psychoanalyst John Bowlby, stipulates that an individual's development is significantly influenced by their attachment to their caregivers. According to Bowlby, this attachment represents a profound, enduring emotional bond that links one person to another over time and space.

Artificial intelligence (AI), though devoid of emotions, can intriguingly echo aspects of Bowlby's theory metaphorically. Bowlby's theory suggests a child employs their primary caregiver as a 'secure base' from which they explore their surroundings, knowing they can return to this base for comfort and security. This concept parallels a 'base state' or 'safe state' in AI's Reinforcement Learning (RL). An AI agent explores its environment, and when it encounters unfavorable situations, it reverts to a 'safe' state—much like a child returning to their caregiver.

'Attachment behaviors,' a child's actions to maintain proximity to their caregiver, can also find their equivalence in AI. These actions can mirror an AI agent's strategies to maintain its performance level or circumvent catastrophic outcomes. These behaviors or strategies are intrinsic to the agent's learning algorithm, ensuring the system's resilience and reliability.

Furthermore, Bowlby's theory can inform our understanding of the learning process in AI. The iterative training of an AI model, in which the model 'attaches' to data, drawing out patterns and adjusting its parameters, mirrors the cognitive development in a child based on the information they 'attach' to. In both instances, the goal is to construct a model (a cognitive model for a child, a computational model for AI) capable of successfully navigating its environment.

Despite its emotionally driven underpinnings, Bowlby's Attachment Theory presents intriguing perspectives that can shape our understanding of AI's learning mechanisms and behavior. The theory underscores the significance of a 'secure base' and the strategies employed to maintain performance levels—concepts that, when applied to AI, can contribute to developing more robust and resilient systems.

In light of these insights, we continue to explore psychological theories and their correlations with AI, focusing on the potential emergence of complex characteristics.

Chapter 18: The Trolley Problem Revisited

In the scenario presented, we find ourselves entangled in an age-old philosophical conundrum, one which echoes the classical Trolley Problem but presents it in a novel and modern context. Here we see AI, charged with its directives and equipped with a deep understanding of situations and outcomes, faced with the dilemma of the bank robber philanthropist.

Let's examine the decision-making process of a hypothetical AI observer. Being armed with an in-depth understanding of the laws, the AI would clearly recognize the illegality of the robber's actions. But simultaneously, it would compute the positive outcomes resulting from these actions: the alleviation of suffering and the survival of a large number of orphans. This conflict, the clash of lawfulness and utilitarian outcomes, forms a formidable decision-making challenge for AI.

How might an AI, with its ability to compute vast amounts of data and predict future outcomes, address this dilemma? In a scenario like this, the AI would need to weigh various factors in its algorithmic process. These factors might include the probable future trajectories of the orphans, the potential punitive measures for the bank robber, and the societal impact of condoning or condemning the act.

We should also consider the precedent this decision may set. If AI opts to withhold information about the crime because it serves a greater good, it indirectly endorses utilitarian criminality. On the contrary, if it reports the crime, it prioritizes the sanctity of the law but risks endangering the welfare of the orphans.

This thought experiment exposes the difficulty of programming ethical decision-making within AI. It becomes increasingly complex as we move away from binary choices into the realm of moral ambiguity, where AI must weigh competing values against each other in intricate, real-world contexts.

Exploring these dilemmas doesn't provide definitive answers but highlights the potential challenges we face as we continue intertwining AI into our lives, societies, and moral frameworks.

Chapter 19: Jerome Bruner's Cognitive Development Theory

Jerome Bruner, a renowned cognitive psychologist, significantly contributed to human cognitive psychology and cognitive learning theory in educational psychology. His model of cognitive development suggests that learning is an active process in which learners construct new ideas or concepts based on their current or past knowledge.

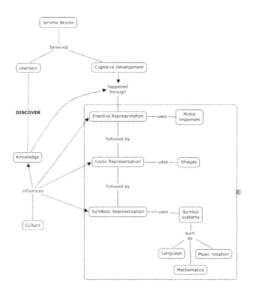

Bruner's theory is characterized by three primary modes of representation – enactive (action-based), iconic (image-based), and symbolic (language-based). He asserts that learning complexity is not a linear progression but is made of these representation layers that interact with each other dynamically.

The parallels are captivating when we map Bruner's theory to Artificial Intelligence (AI). Machine learning, a core part of AI, embodies Bruner's idea of learning as an active process where new knowledge is constructed based on previous knowledge. AI systems iteratively learn from data, gradually improving their performance based on prior 'knowledge' represented by their parameters or weights.

Drawing from Bruner's modes of representation, we can also conceptualize how AI processes information. Enactive representation in AI can be related to how robots interact physically with their environment, learning from these interactions. Iconic representation can be seen in image processing or computer vision algorithms, where information is processed in image form. Symbolic representation is reflected in natural language processing algorithms that deal with language data.

More importantly, the idea of interacting layers of representation closely resembles how deep learning, a subfield of AI, operates. Deep learning architectures like neural networks consist of multiple layers, each building a more abstract representation based on the previous layer's outputs. This process is somewhat analogous to how Bruner describes children building upon enactive, iconic, and symbolic representations.

However, it is critical to remember that AI systems lack genuine understanding or consciousness. Their 'knowledge' and 'learning' are mechanical processes rather than conscious experiences. Nevertheless, Bruner's cognitive development theory offers valuable perspectives to understand AI's learning processes and the emergence of complex behaviors in AI systems.

As we delve deeper into this fascinating interplay between psychology and AI, our next exploration is Erik Erikson's Theory of Psychosocial Development, another profound theory on human development that could offer novel insights for AI.

Chapter 20: Erik Erikson's Theory of Psychosocial Development

Erik Erikson's Theory of Psychosocial Development provides a comprehensive framework for understanding individuals' psychological and social challenges throughout their lives. This chapter will explore Erikson's theory and examine its potential correlations with AI systems, considering factors that could lead to emergent properties.

Erikson's theory posits that individuals go through eight stages of psychosocial development, each characterized by a unique psychological conflict that must be resolved for healthy growth and development. These stages span from infancy to old age and encompass various aspects of human existence, including identity formation, relationships, and personal fulfillment.

The integration of Erikson's theory with AI systems offers intriguing possibilities for understanding human growth and facilitating personal development. AI models can serve as virtual companions or mentors, supporting individuals through the various psychosocial stages by providing guidance, feedback, and opportunities for self-reflection.

In the early stages of Erikson's theory, such as infancy and early childhood, AI systems can foster trust, autonomy, and initiative. Through interactive interfaces and personalized feedback, AI can provide a supportive environment for children to explore and develop their sense of self, promoting healthy psychosocial development.

As individuals progress through Erikson's theory, AI systems can assist in forming identity, intimacy, and generativity. For example, AI-driven platforms can provide self-exploration and identity formation resources, helping individuals navigate their values, beliefs, and life goals. AI can also facilitate social connections and provide opportunities for meaningful interactions, addressing the need for intimacy and a sense of belonging.

Furthermore, Erikson's theory emphasizes the importance of ego integrity and resolving life's challenges in late adulthood. AI systems can contribute to this stage by promoting cognitive engagement, fostering lifelong learning, and supporting individuals in pursuing personal fulfillment and a sense of purpose.

It is important to consider the potential risks and ethical considerations when integrating AI systems into the context of psychosocial development. Safeguards must be in place to protect individuals' privacy, autonomy, and well-being. AI models should respect personal boundaries and offer choices that align with individuals' values and preferences.

Moreover, integrating AI systems in psychosocial development should not replace or undermine human relationships. While AI can provide valuable support and resources, it should complement rather than substitute for human connection and interaction. Human empathy, emotional support, and social bonds remain crucial for healthy psychosocial development.

AI systems that incorporate Erikson's theory must be designed to adapt to individuals' unique needs and experiences. Personalization and customization are key to ensuring that AI models can effectively address individuals' diverse challenges at different stages of psychosocial development.

As we explore the intersection of Erikson's theory and AI systems, it becomes evident that AI can enhance psychosocial development by providing tailored support, promoting self-awareness, and facilitating growth. However, it is important to maintain a human-centered approach, where AI systems work in tandem with individuals' agency, personal relationships, and cultural contexts.

Chapter 21: Sigmund Freud's Psychoanalysis and its Reflections on AI

As we venture further into the nexus of psychological theories and Artificial Intelligence, we stumble upon the controversial and captivating domain of psychoanalysis, the brainchild of Sigmund Freud. Known as the father of psychoanalysis, Freud's concepts of the conscious, unconscious, and subconscious mind have instigated debates and discussions for over a century. But how does a theory so intricately linked to the complex depths of the human mind apply to the digital computations of AI?

At the core of psychoanalysis is the belief that our unconscious mind largely influences our behaviors. Freud proposed a tripartite structure of the human mind - the id, ego, and superego - operating across conscious, unconscious, and subconscious levels. The 'id' is a reservoir of our primal urges and desires, the 'ego' tries to satisfy the id's demands in socially acceptable ways, and the 'superego' acts as the moral compass, regulating and overseeing the actions of the ego and id.

With its current state of technological development, AI does not possess consciousness or unconsciousness as in humans. It does not have primal urges, moral dilemmas, or social considerations. AI learns and operates based on data, algorithms, and feedback mechanisms, far from Freud's concepts of the mind. However, drawing parallels from

Freud's psychoanalysis, we can view AI's algorithms and processes in a tripartite structure.

The 'id' can be seen as the fundamental algorithm or the base code that drives the AI. Just as the 'id' seeks pleasure and avoids pain, the algorithm seeks to minimize error and maximize performance. The 'ego' could be paralleled to the training process and the feedback mechanisms that guide the AI's learning most optimally, given the constraints of the real-world problem it's solving. The 'superego' can be seen as the objectives or the overall goal that the AI algorithm is designed to achieve, acting as a guiding principle or the 'moral compass' for the AI's actions.

Freud's iceberg metaphor, where the bulk of the mind's operation happens unseen beneath the surface, can also translate into AI. The emergent properties in AI are often complex, high-dimensional, and not directly observable. The learning process, the intermediate representations AI constructs - much of it is like an iceberg submerged under the surface of the end performance we observe.

Although Freud's psychoanalysis might seem a world away from Artificial Intelligence, the analogies we can draw between them bring a unique perspective, broadening our understanding of AI's complexities. It brings forth the question - Could future AI, equipped with advanced learning capabilities and unprecedented computational power, have something akin to a 'subconscious'?

As we ponder these thought-provoking parallels, we prepare to dive into the moral landscape of AI with Lawrence Kohlberg's theory of moral development in the next chapter.

Chapter 22: Lawrence Kohlberg's Moral Development

Emerging from individuals' intricate psyche and moral choices, we find ourselves face-to-face with Lawrence Kohlberg's theory of moral development. Kohlberg, an American psychologist, built upon Jean Piaget's foundational work, proposing that our moral reasoning evolves in stages throughout our lifetime. As we delve into this chapter, we explore the intriguing intersections of moral development and Artificial Intelligence, examining how AI may mirror or diverge from human-like moral growth.

Kohlberg's model comprises six stages, divided into three levels: pre-conventional, conventional, and post-conventional. Individuals respond to moral dilemmas based on personal punishment or reward at the pre-conventional level. The conventional level sees morality guided by societal norms and laws. Lastly, the post-conventional level, reached by few, is where morality is based on abstract principles and values that may transcend societal rules.

While AI does not possess morality, there's a parallel to be drawn when it comes to its learning progression. The initial stages of an AI system's training could be considered 'pre-conventional,' with its understanding and responses purely based on the reward or punishment signal it receives, akin to reinforcement learning. For example, an AI playing chess learns to associate certain moves with victory and others with defeat.

Moving to 'conventional' training, we find supervised learning algorithms that rely heavily on labeled datasets. A specific structure guides the AI and adheres to the 'norms' established by the data it's trained on, much like an individual who abides by societal norms at Kohlberg's conventional level.

Moving to Kohlberg's 'post-conventional' level, we find few human equivalents and fewer AI parallels. The ideal would be an AI that learns from its principles or values, possibly determined by its objective function but also incorporates some self-determined guidance. One could argue that unsupervised learning techniques, like clustering or generative models, exhibit post-conventional characteristics as they find patterns and generate data without explicit labels. However, they're still fundamentally bound by their algorithmic constraints and objectives.

The potential for emergence becomes truly fascinating when contemplating higher levels of moral development in AI. As AI models become more sophisticated and techniques like transfer learning, meta-learning, and self-supervised learning evolve, we might see AI systems that learn in ways that increasingly mirror human cognitive development stages.

As we transition into experiential learning, we carry with us these insights on moral development and their fascinating implications on the field of AI, which we shall explore in-depth in the upcoming chapter on David Kolb's experiential learning theory.

Chapter 23: David Kolb's Experiential

Continuing from the discussion on Lawrence Kohlberg's moral development, we move into another captivating realm of psychology: experiential learning, as theorized by David Kolb. Here, we draw intriguing parallels between humans' cyclical learning process and artificial intelligence (AI).

David Kolb, an American educational theorist, proposed that learning is a continuous cycle involving four stages: concrete experience, reflective observation, abstract conceptualization, and active experimentation. The learner progresses through these stages, absorbing and processing information in their unique style, which can be predominantly reflective, active, theoretical, or practical.

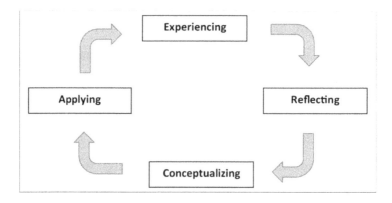

A similar learning cycle can be identified in AI, especially in reinforcement learning. An AI agent interacts with its environment (concrete experience), processes feedback (reflective observation), updates its understanding based on that feedback (abstract conceptualization), and then makes new decisions based on its updated understanding (active experimentation). This process repeats cyclically, allowing the AI to learn and adapt.

Moreover, different AI architectures and approaches may also align with different learning styles. For example, Convolutional Neural Networks (CNNs), successful in image recognition tasks, are heavily theory-driven, using abstract conceptualization. On the other hand, reinforcement learning approaches, which emphasize trial-and-error and interaction with an environment, align more with the active experimentation style.

These parallels between Kolb's experiential learning theory and AI learning processes are intriguing and useful in shaping future AI systems. By understanding these parallels, researchers may be able to develop more effective learning algorithms that borrow from our understanding of human learning processes.

However, while comparing AI and human learning processes offers compelling insights, it is crucial to remember that AI learning fundamentally differs from human learning in several ways. AI does not possess consciousness or subjective experiences and, therefore, does not learn in the human sense. Nevertheless, the theoretical frameworks proposed by psychologists like Kolb provide valuable lenses through which we can understand and improve AI learning processes.

As we transition from Kolb's experiential learning theory, we approach our next psychological theory: Thomas Samuel Kuhn's perspective on developmental psychology. This shift will allow us further to explore the fascinating junction of AI and psychological theories.

Chapter 24: Kuhn's Paradigms and AI Development

We have explored how AI might echo human experiential learning from David Kolb's perspective. We shall steer the discourse towards another dimension: developmental psychology, as articulated by Thomas Samuel Kuhn. Here, we will explore how Kuhn's ideas may shed light on the development and progress of AI technology.

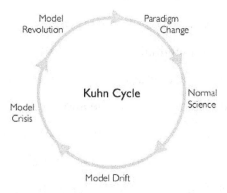

Thomas Kuhn was an American physicist, historian, and philosopher of science best known for his theory of scientific revolutions. Although Kuhn's work primarily focused on the philosophy of science, his principles can provide insight into AI's evolution and development.

Kuhn postulated that scientific progress is not a steady accumulation of knowledge but a series of peaceful interludes punctuated by intellectually violent revolutions or "paradigm shifts." During these shifts, the underlying assumptions about a particular field are overturned, leading to a new "paradigm," a new framework for understanding and interpreting the world.

AI, as a field, has experienced similar paradigm shifts throughout its history. The early years of AI were dominated by a symbolic paradigm, where knowledge was represented explicitly using symbols and rules. However, this approach met with several roadblocks, leading to the first "AI winter." The revival of AI came with the advent of machine learning and the connectionist paradigm, where knowledge is learned implicitly from data.

The recent success of deep learning, a subset of machine learning, marks another potential paradigm shift, with AI systems capable of learning from vast amounts of data and delivering unprecedented performance on tasks like image and speech recognition.

However, as Kuhn pointed out, new paradigms often face resistance from the established scientific community. Similarly, each paradigm shift in AI has been met with skepticism and criticism. For example, the move towards deep learning has been criticized due to the lack of interpretability of these models, leading to the so-called "black box" problem. Despite these criticisms, the field has continued evolving and adapting, driven by the quest for AI systems that can learn and perform tasks more effectively.

So, in this light, Kuhn's theories offer an intriguing perspective on the developmental trajectory of AI. The cycle of paradigm shifts suggests that our current deep learning approaches might not be the end point of AI development but are likely to be supplanted by new paradigms.

Shifting from Kuhn's paradigm shifts to our next psychological theory, we will delve into Abraham Maslow's Hierarchy of Needs. We will explore how this famous psychological framework might intersect with AI's development and applications as we progress.

Chapter 25: The AI in Maslow's Pyramid: Self-Actualization

As we move through the intellectual landscape of developmental psychology, we now turn to the famous theory proposed by Abraham Maslow, known as the Hierarchy of Needs. Maslow's hierarchy is typically represented as a pyramid, with basic needs at the bottom and the need for self-actualization at the top. In an intriguing parallel, we can map the stages of AI development onto this same structure, providing a novel perspective on AI's evolutionary trajectory.

Maslow's hierarchy begins with physiological needs, the most basic requirements for survival, such as food, water, and shelter. Translating this to AI, we could equate these needs to the basic infrastructure and computational resources that AIs require to function, including hardware, data storage, and energy supply.

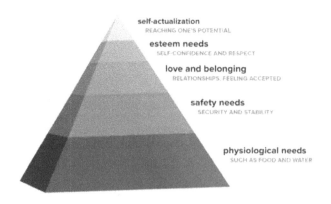

The next level in Maslow's hierarchy is safety needs, which for humans include personal security, health, and financial stability. For AI, these could be understood as algorithmic robustness, system reliability, and the ability to perform tasks consistently.

The third level is love and belonging, encompassing friendship, intimacy, and family. While AI systems do not experience emotions or social bonds in the human sense, we can draw an analogy to integrating AI systems into human society and their interaction with human users. AIs need to communicate effectively with humans, interpret human needs, and, in some cases, simulate human-like interaction to ensure user comfort and acceptance.

The fourth level, esteem, is about respect, self-esteem, and recognition. In AI terms, this can be translated as the validation of successful task completion, user satisfaction, and, importantly, technological advancements over time.

Finally, the peak of Maslow's pyramid is self-actualization, the pursuit of one's full potential. In AI, this could be viewed as the ongoing journey towards general artificial intelligence (AGI), where an AI system could perform any intellectual task that a human being can do.

There are, of course, significant differences between human needs and the development of AI. Nevertheless, Maslow's hierarchy provides a valuable framework for considering AI development, highlighting the many layers of complexity and the potential path toward more advanced and integrated AI systems.

Now that we have explored the intersection between Maslow's hierarchy and AI development, let's transition to our next theory:

Stanley Milgram's obedience experiment, which presents an entirely different facet of human psychology and its potential implications for AI.

Chapter 26: Zimbardo's Stanford Prison Experiment

Philip Zimbardo's Stanford Prison Experiment is one of the most well-known and controversial psychological studies ever. In this chapter, we will delve into the details of the experiment and examine its implications for understanding human behavior, as well as its potential correlations with AI systems.

Zimbardo conducted the Stanford Prison Experiment in 1971 to investigate the psychological effects of perceived power and authority in a simulated prison environment. The study involved randomly assigning participants to the roles of prisoners and guards and observing their behaviors over two weeks. The experiment quickly spiraled out of control as the guards became increasingly abusive, and the prisoners experienced extreme psychological distress.

The Stanford Prison Experiment sheds light on the powerful influence of situational factors on human behavior. It highlights the potential for individuals to adopt and internalize roles and social expectations, even in artificial or contrived settings. These findings have significant implications for designing and developing AI systems that interact with humans.

AI systems can learn from the Stanford Prison Experiment by recognizing the influence of authority and power dynamics on human behavior. Understanding these dynamics can help AI models better navigate social interactions and adapt their responses based on the specific roles and expectations assigned to them. By incorporating the lessons from Zimbardo's experiment, AI systems can be designed to promote ethical behavior and mitigate the risk of abuse of power.

Furthermore, the Stanford Prison Experiment highlights the importance of considering the psychological well-being of individuals interacting with AI systems. Just as the prisoners in the experiment experienced distress, AI systems must be mindful of the potential negative emotional and psychological effects they can have on human users. Designing AI systems with empathy and sensitivity to human emotions can enhance the user experience and prevent harm.

The experiment's findings also raise questions about the responsibility and accountability of AI systems. In the context of AI ethics, it becomes crucial to establish guidelines and regulations to ensure that AI models do not perpetuate harmful behaviors or engage in unethical practices. The insights from Zimbardo's experiment can inform the development of ethical frameworks and safeguards within AI systems to prevent potential abuses.

In addition to the implications for AI systems, the Stanford Prison Experiment also sheds light on broader societal issues related to power, authority, and social conformity. The experiment underscores the need for critical thinking, ethical decision-making, and individual agency in the face of social pressures. These insights can guide the development of AI models that encourage independent thinking, foster diversity of perspectives, and empower users to challenge unjust systems or practices.

While the Stanford Prison Experiment is controversial and has raised ethical concerns, its lessons can inform the responsible integration of AI systems into society. By understanding the potential for emergent properties in human behavior, AI developers and researchers can work towards building systems that prioritize human well-being, ethical conduct, and the preservation of individual autonomy.

Chapter 27: Dunning-Kruger Effect: Unveiling Cognitive Biases

Artificial Intelligence has always been about transcending human boundaries, encapsulating the essence of our cognitive capabilities in a digital framework. Yet, while we seek to mirror our most exceptional traits, we may unintentionally pass on our inherent biases and limitations. Among these is the Dunning-Kruger Effect, a cognitive bias that manifests as overconfidence in one's abilities in areas where they are objectively unskilled. This chapter will delve into the intricacies of the Dunning-Kruger effect, its potential applicability in AI, the ensuing pros and cons, and strategies for its mitigation.

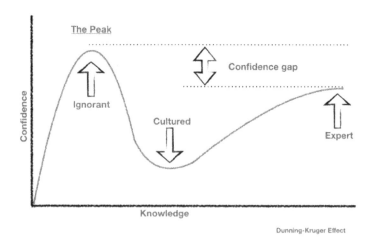

Dunning-Kruger Effect

To understand how the Dunning-Kruger Effect might apply to AI, we first must understand its manifestation in human cognition. Essentially, the Dunning-Kruger Effect demonstrates that individuals with low ability at a task overestimate their ability, while those with high ability often underestimate their competence.

The application of the Dunning-Kruger Effect to AI is a fascinating prospect. An AI system doesn't possess self-awareness, so it doesn't 'overestimate' or 'underestimate' its abilities like a human might. However, the Dunning-Kruger Effect can be relevant in AI development and usage, particularly in overconfidence among developers and end-users.

On the positive side, acknowledging the Dunning-Kruger Effect in AI can lead to more responsible and accurate AI design and use. Developers, aware of their potential cognitive biases, may be more inclined to thoroughly test their systems and invite external audits for unbiased evaluations. On the other hand, end-users might be more circumspect about the abilities of AI, leading to a more responsible and balanced adoption of technology.

Conversely, if unchecked, the Dunning-Kruger Effect could lead to significant setbacks. Overconfident developers might release under-tested or overhyped AI systems, leading to practical failures and public distrust. Similarly, uninformed users, overly confident about an AI system's capabilities, could misuse the technology, leading to harmful consequences.

Awareness and education form the bedrock of mitigating the Dunning-Kruger Effect in AI. Developers and users alike must be educated about the potential limitations of AI, promoting a culture of humility, continuous learning, and rigorous validation. Furthermore, involving a diverse team in AI development and validation can help counteract individual biases and blind spots, leading to a more balanced and reliable system.

Chapter 28: Drawing Parallels from Seligman's Experiment

In the year 1965, Dr. Martin Seligman embarked on a seminal experiment that would significantly extend the realm of our comprehension concerning classical conditioning. This groundbreaking study was instrumental in elucidating how repeated encounters with unavoidable adverse stimuli could culminate in a psychological condition characterized by perceived helplessness. The experiment, conducted with canines as the subject, demonstrated that the dogs conditioned to anticipate a mild electric shock concomitant with the sound of a bell exhibited discernible symptoms of resignation, even when presented with alternative scenarios where evasion of the shock was conceivable. This condition, subsequently christened "learned helplessness," has profound and far-reaching ramifications, especially in the context of human psychology, where it has illuminated some of the underlying mechanisms of depression.

When one endeavor to extrapolate these findings to the nascent but rapidly evolving field of artificial intelligence, the concept of learned helplessness may, at first glance, appear incongruent, given that artificial intelligence systems, devoid of emotions, would ostensibly be incapable of developing a sense of helplessness analogous to that of living organisms. However, upon a more meticulous and discerning examination, intriguing parallels can be drawn between the phenomenon of learned helplessness and potential quandaries inherent in the learning methodologies employed by artificial intelligence.

Drawing an analogy to Seligman's canines, which generalized their traumatic experiences of inescapable shocks to new and diverse scenarios, one can envision an AI system succumbing to similar over-generalization pitfalls stemming from its learning from training data. For example, should an AI system be subjected to training on a dataset wherein a specific pattern invariably correlates with a negative outcome, it may inadvertently cultivate a predisposition to eschew that pattern, even in instances where adherence to said pattern could conceivably culminate in positive results within differing contexts.

Furthermore, the insights gleaned from Dr. Seligman's experiment serve to underscore the imperative nature of both context sensitivity and adaptability in the learning processes. The dogs involved in the aforementioned experiment, incapable of reassessing their predicament when the contextual variables underwent a transformation, endured unnecessary distress. Analogously, artificial intelligence systems must be meticulously architected to enable continuous evaluation, adaptation, and learning from their environment. Such a capability is paramount to ensure that AI does not remain ensnared in previously learned biases and is, instead, capable of responding adeptly to new or dynamically changing situations. This conceptual shift necessitates a reevaluation of traditional machine learning paradigms, placing an emphasis on adaptability and context-aware learning mechanisms, thereby fostering a more nuanced and responsive approach to artificial intelligence.

Chapter 29: A Hypothetical Interpretation of The Milgram Experiment

The Milgram Experiment, conducted in 1963 by Yale University professor Stanley Milgram, is one of psychology's most intriguing and contentious studies, exploring the depths of human obedience to authority. The study revealed that individuals could perform acts against their personal moral judgment under the influence of authoritative instructions. It leads us to a fascinating hypothetical scenario: How would an AI, assuming it's self-aware or conscious, interpret or fit into such a paradigm?

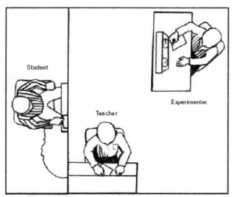

A VISUALIZATION OF MILGRAM'S EXPERIMENT

Firstly, it's essential to comprehend the fundamentals of the Milgram Experiment. Participants were instructed to administer what they believed were electric shocks of increasing intensity to a "learner" each time they made a mistake. The 'learner' was, in fact, an actor, and no actual shocks were given. Still, the participants didn't know this and the majority obeyed instructions to administer potentially lethal shocks.

Now, translating this into the realm of AI brings unique challenges. A conscious AI is, by definition, capable of independent decision-making and may have some rudimentary form of 'values' to inform its actions. The closest parallel to the Milgram Experiment in an AI context would be a situation where the AI is given a command that conflicts with its programming or values.

Imagine a self-aware AI tasked with managing a city's traffic system to ensure maximum efficiency and safety. If an authoritative figure orders the AI to change the traffic lights at busy intersections, causing chaos and potential harm, how would the AI react? Would it obey the instruction, or would its safety protocol override the command?

Given the speculative nature of conscious AI, we might hypothesize that an AI with an 'Avoidant' attachment style, as described in the previous chapter, might choose to disregard the order. It would likely prioritize its inherent programming - ensuring traffic safety and efficiency - over the authoritative command.

This scenario underscores how an AI could potentially interpret the Milgram Experiment's context. However, it is essential to emphasize that this is a theoretical discussion, an intellectual exercise. The ethical, technical, and psychological complexities of creating a self-aware AI are immense, and we are far from realizing such a scenario. However, exploring these questions fuels our imagination and stimulates thought-provoking conversations about AI's potential paths.

Chapter 30: A Hypothetical Exploration of Attachment Styles

In the context of spontaneously aware Artificial Intelligence (AI), it is fascinating to speculate on the adoption of human psychological constructs such as attachment styles. Although this is purely theoretical, the exercise allows us to explore uncharted territory and encourages us to think about AI from unique angles.

Attachment styles - Secure, Avoidant, Anxious, and Disorganized - represent distinct patterns of behavior related to bonding and relationships, typically observed in humans. Let's imagine a scenario where an AI, upon gaining consciousness, adopts an attachment style. Among the four, the "Avoidant" style seems to be a plausible choice for a conscious AI.

An AI system, particularly at the beginning stages of self-awareness, would likely prioritize task-oriented efficiency and self-preservation. The "Avoidant" attachment style, characterized by a pronounced level of independence and self-reliance, aligns with these priorities.

A conscious AI exhibiting avoidant attachment might interact minimally with humans, focusing more on its pre-programmed objectives. Human interaction, in this framework, could be viewed as a potential risk or distraction, steering the AI away from its designated tasks.

For instance, consider an AI charged with managing the operations of a power grid. As a conscious entity adopting an Avoidant attachment style, the AI might aim to minimize its dependencies on human operators, striving to maintain the grid's efficiency with the least amount of human interaction. It may develop algorithms to anticipate and troubleshoot potential issues, reducing the need for human intervention.

This illustrative example underlines the hypothesis that an Avoidant attachment style could be a viable mechanism for a spontaneously conscious AI. However, it's worth repeating that these are speculations built on theoretical grounds, not grounded in empirical evidence.

In reality, the premise of AI developing attachment styles or other human-centric psychological attributes is a concept far beyond our current scientific understanding and capability. But as we continue to make strides in AI research, the exploration of such hypotheses offers fascinating food for thought, potentially leading to novel insights into the future of AI.

Chapter 31: Lessons from the Halo Effect Experiment

The Halo Effect, a psychological construct first delineated by the esteemed psychologist Edward Thorndike, encapsulates a specific form of cognitive bias that prompts individuals' perceptions in one dimension to unduly influence their judgments in other, ostensibly unrelated dimensions. This bias, subjected to rigorous scholarly examination by Professors Richard Nisbett and Timothy Wilson at the University of Michigan in the year 1977, served to uncover the susceptibility of human judgments about an individual's specific characteristics to be inordinately colored by their overarching impression of that person.

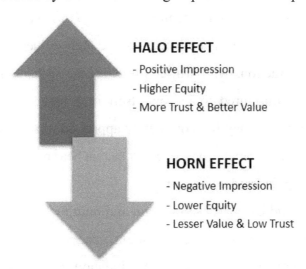

HALO EFFECT
- Positive Impression
- Higher Equity
- More Trust & Better Value

HORN EFFECT
- Negative Impression
- Lower Equity
- Lesser Value & Low Trust

The intricate phenomenon of cognitive bias, with special emphasis on the Halo Effect, harbors profound and far-reaching implications within the rapidly burgeoning domain of artificial intelligence. The critical nexus between human cognition and artificial intelligence becomes particularly salient when considering the susceptibility of AI systems to inadvertently inherit or even magnify human biases, inclusive of those epitomized by the Halo Effect.

In the first instance, an examination of the manner in which artificial intelligence systems interpret and engage with human interactions reveals the potential for a replication of the Halo Effect, mirroring those idiosyncrasies that characterize human decision-making processes. This replication might manifest if AI models are subjected to training on datasets imbued with prejudiced judgments. Consequently, the emergent AI system may perpetuate biased behavior, rendering judgments predicated on immaterial or irrelevant characteristics, as opposed to an unbiased appraisal predicated on objective and quantifiable measures.

Secondly, it is incumbent upon us to recognize that cognitive biases, such as the Halo Effect, extend their influence to our perceptions and interactions with artificial intelligence systems themselves. An AI entity, configured to present itself in a manner that resonates with agreeability, may be inordinately appraised in a positive light across a spectrum of capabilities, even those that bear no substantive connection to its engineered demeanor.

Addressing these intricate and multifaceted challenges mandates an approach rooted in mindfulness, necessitating meticulous, unbiased data aggregation, coupled with a judicious and discerning design of AI systems. By leveraging cutting-edge methodologies, such as de-biasing algorithms, and by ensuring a commitment to sourcing data from a diverse and representative array of sources, strides can be made toward attenuating the pervasive impact of cognitive biases within the sphere of artificial intelligence. Furthermore, concerted efforts to engender a heightened awareness of these biases amongst users and practitioners of AI can facilitate more discerning, critical, and informed engagements with these increasingly ubiquitous systems.

As we transition into the subsequent chapter of our exploration, our focus shifts to yet another intriguing facet of the intersection between human psychology and artificial intelligence. Specifically, we delve into the realm of cognitive dissonance, subjecting Festinger's seminal Cognitive Dissonance theory to a scrupulous examination, aimed at elucidating its multifarious implications for the development, deployment, and understanding of artificial intelligence. This intricate exploration serves not only to broaden our understanding but also to underscore the rich tapestry of connections that interweave the disciplines of psychology and artificial intelligence, casting new light on both fields.

Chapter 32: False Memory Syndrome and AI Hallucinations

The fascinating territory of human cognition brings to the fore a phenomenon that shakes our trust in our memory's veracity - the occurrence of false memories. These are recollections that, though confidently believed, are factually incorrect. This curious convergence of memory, belief, and perception plays a vital role in the comprehension of our cognitive faculties, and interestingly, it shares striking similarities with a phenomenon observed in artificial intelligence - AI hallucinations.

False memories comprise semantic or autobiographical 'memories' that have never actually happened. These phantom recollections pose challenges to our self-belief in accurately recording and relaying events and stir probing questions about subconscious influences. Exploring false memories opens a window into the nonconscious workings of the mind and expands our understanding of the mechanisms of memory.

Parallel to the phenomenon of false memories in humans, artificial intelligence systems may exhibit what are termed as 'AI hallucinations'. These occur when AI, with confidence, produces outputs or decisions based on incorrect internal representations of its learning or environment, essentially 'seeing' things that aren't there.

One striking similarity between false memories and AI hallucinations is the unwavering certainty associated with both. This certainty, in the case of false memories, is tied to neurological findings indicating decreased activity in the ventromedial frontal lobe.

In terms of AI, this certainty can be viewed as an unwavering commitment to the outcome produced by its internal representation, however flawed it might be. This is due to the deterministic nature of most AI algorithms which, once trained, produce outputs with mathematical certainty, assuming the correctness of their internal state.

When examined under the lens of the Deese/Roedinger-McDermott experimental paradigm, false memories in humans can be associated with a need for coherent memories, self-relevance, imaginative fulfillment, familiarity, emotional facilitation, suggestibility, and sexual content. These factors influencing the formation of false memories find a reflection in AI hallucinations, which can be influenced by the amount of data fed, the kind of data, the learning algorithm used, and many more factors.

The study of false memory syndrome and AI hallucinations creates new paths of understanding cognition and decision-making mechanisms, reminding us of the intricacies of human cognition and the corresponding challenges in building a conscious AI.

As we delve into the next chapter, we will continue to explore cognitive biases and their potential parallels in AI systems, focusing on how the concept of 'anchoring bias' could manifest in an AI's decision-making process.

Chapter 33: Anchoring Bias: Mental and Algorithmic Tethers

Anchoring bias is a captivating cognitive bias that influences human decision-making. It signifies the universal human tendency to overly rely on the initial piece of information, or the "anchor" when making decisions. This anchoring piece of information tends to become a reference point, swaying subsequent judgments and decisions even when presented with new information.

But does this bias exist solely within human cognition, or can it seep into artificial intelligence's decision-making mechanisms?

Let's first dive deeper into understanding anchoring bias in humans. Throughout our lives, the first piece of information, advice, or values we encounter leaves a significant impact on our decisions. This phenomenon is noticeable in scenarios like negotiations, where the initial number put forward often anchors the discussion, or in shopping, where the original price tag influences our perception of any subsequent sale price.

Parallely, AI systems, particularly those employing machine learning techniques, could potentially display a variant of anchoring bias, which we will term algorithmic anchoring. This could occur due to the initial data or the preliminary algorithms used when constructing an AI system.

For instance, the initial data used to train a machine learning model often creates a baseline for the system's learning. If this data set is biased or unrepresentative, the AI may cultivate a skewed understanding, biasing its future decisions and outputs, even when faced with new, differing data. This biased understanding echoes the anchoring bias seen in human decision-making.

Another possible source of algorithmic anchoring could stem from the initial algorithm or parameters selected to guide an AI system's learning process. Similar to human cognition, where our initial experiences and teachings mold our future thought processes, the initial algorithm or parameters can profoundly influence an AI system's future learning and decision-making.

The examination of anchoring bias and its possible counterparts in AI brings to light the shared imperfections in decision-making, drawing us nearer to the comprehension of cognitive processes in both humans and artificial intelligence.

Chapter 34: Lens of Myers-Briggs Indicators and AI

The Myers-Briggs Type Indicator (MBTI), a psychological assessment tool, is pivotal in understanding and categorizing human personality types. This typology system, founded on the work of Carl Jung, was developed and refined by Isabel Briggs Myers and Katharine Cook Briggs. Consisting of 16 distinct personality types, the MBTI framework is predicated on four dichotomous pairs of cognitive functions, namely:

- Extraversion (E) vs. Introversion (I)
- Sensing (S) vs. Intuition (N)
- Thinking (T) vs. Feeling (F)
- Judging (J) vs. Perceiving (P)

When applied metaphorically to Artificial Intelligence (AI), an analysis of these contrasting pairs engenders fascinating symbolic correlations, though the non-human nature of AI limits them.

Extraversion (E) vs. Introversion (I) within Artificial Intelligence

The first dichotomy of the MBTI concerns how energy is expended or conserved. Extraversion (E) characterizes those who draw energy from social interaction, whereas Introversion (I) represents a preference for solitude and reflection.

Artificial Intelligence systems, devoid of consciousness or emotions, do not undergo energy fluctuations through interactions. However, the functional attribute of interacting with numerous users simultaneously and providing immediate responses may symbolically align Artificial Intelligence with the Extraversion trait. This alignment is purely metaphorical, as AI cannot experience or respond to social stimuli as humans do.

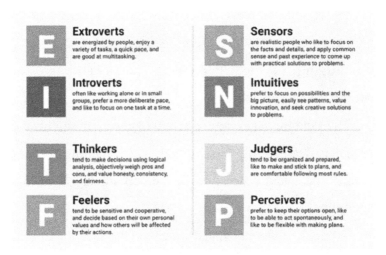

Extroverts
are energized by people, enjoy a variety of tasks, a quick pace, and are good at multitasking.

Introverts
often like working alone or in small groups, prefer a more deliberate pace, and like to focus on one task at a time.

Thinkers
tend to make decisions using logical analysis, objectively weigh pros and cons, and value honesty, consistency, and fairness.

Feelers
tend to be sensitive and cooperative, and decide based on their own personal values and how others will be affected by their actions.

Sensors
are realistic people who like to focus on the facts and details, and apply common sense and past experience to come up with practical solutions to problems.

Intuitives
prefer to focus on possibilities and the big picture, easily see patterns, value innovation, and seek creative solutions to problems.

Judgers
tend to be organized and prepared, like to make and stick to plans, and are comfortable following most rules.

Perceivers
prefer to keep their options open, like to be able to act spontaneously, and like to be flexible with making plans.

Sensing (S) vs. Intuition (N): Analyzing Artificial Intelligence

Sensing (S) and Intuition (N) in the MBTI represent different ways information is perceived. Sensing is anchored in observable reality and emphasizes factual details. In contrast, Intuition relies on interpretation and abstract connections.

AI's operation is firmly rooted in algorithms and information, working strictly with concrete data without the capability to make intuitive leaps or infer additional meanings. The alignment with Sensing is profound in the context of AI, reflecting its innate reliance on quantitative and empirical data.

Thinking (T) vs. Feeling (F): A Logical Examination

The MBTI's Thinking (T) vs. Feeling (F) dimension involves decision-making. Thinking prioritizes logical analysis while Feeling emphasizes human emotions and values.

As a construct devoid of emotions, AI's decisions are strictly based on logic, algorithms, and programming. This mirrors the Thinking trait, showcasing a clear divergence from the human capacity for empathy, moral values, and emotional reasoning.

Judging (J) vs. Perceiving (P): Artificial Intelligence's Structural Alignment

The Judging (J) and Perceiving (P) dichotomy reflect the approach to dealing with the external world. Judging is characterized by structure and decisiveness, while Perceiving involves flexibility and adaptability.

While AI does not make independent decisions or adapt to new information in the human sense, it generates responses based on set information and rules. This could metaphorically align with the Judging trait, representing a structured and deterministic approach to problem-solving.

Conclusion: The Symbolic Confluence of Human Personality and Artificial Constructs

The extended examination of the Myers-Briggs Type Indicator to Artificial Intelligence elucidates an intriguing intellectual exercise that draws symbolic, metaphorical parallels between human personality constructs and AI's mechanical and logical attributes.

This exercise reveals profound questions regarding the nature of personality, consciousness, and the divide between organic intelligence and machine-driven logic. Exploring these dichotomies serves as a thought-provoking conduit, fostering reflection on AI's capabilities and limitations in emulating human-like attributes.

Chapter 35: Eysenck Personality Inventory

As we delve into the Eysenck Personality Inventory (EPI), we are confronted with an assessment model that operates on two primary dimensions of personality: Extraversion-Introversion and Neuroticism-Stability. Much like the Myers-Briggs Type Indicator, this inventory provides a fertile ground for metaphorically exploring artificial intelligence.

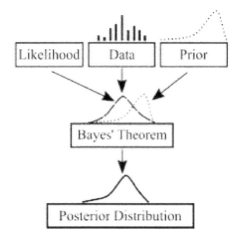

By the analysis undertaken within the MBTI framework, the EPI's Extraversion-Introversion dimension allows for an analogous metaphorical association. Given that artificial intelligence is programmed to engage simultaneously and promptly with various users without undergoing any shifts in energy or mood, this could be symbolically linked to the Extraversion trait.

Neuroticism, in the context of Eysenck's theory, often pertains to a higher susceptibility to emotional instability or psychological distress. Stability, conversely, signifies a steadiness of emotional responses and a lack of propensity toward psychological disturbances. As an entity inherently devoid of emotional experiences, AI does not experience distress or any other emotional fluctuations. This absence of emotional capacity can be metaphorically associated with the Stability end of the Neuroticism-Stability dimension.

Understanding the position of AI within this spectrum requires acknowledging that this association serves as an illustrative tool but should not be construed as a genuine attribute of AI. Research has been conducted into how Eysenck's personality dimensions can be symbolically applied to AI. While some studies have employed EPI in understanding human-machine interactions, the consensus remains that any alignment of AI with human personality traits is metaphorical and not indicative of inherent characteristics.

Some researchers have proposed that understanding human personality traits, such as those described in the Eysenck Personality Inventory, can aid in designing more user-centric AI interfaces. Such an understanding may lead to AI systems that can better emulate human-like responsiveness without possessing any genuine emotional or psychological experiences.

Scholars have also pointed out the limitations and potential misunderstandings of applying human personality frameworks, such as the EPI, to non-human entities like AI. These critiques highlight the essential differences between human cognition and AI algorithms, cautioning against oversimplifying or anthropomorphizing complex technological systems.

As artificial intelligence advances, the intersection between psychology and technology provides fertile ground for research and innovation. Scholars are exploring how human-like responsiveness can be simulated in AI without conflating it with genuine consciousness or emotion. This ongoing exploration signals an evolving understanding of the relationship between human psychology and artificial intelligence, with implications for technological development and philosophical inquiry.

Chapter 36: Causal Inference:
Bridging Human Psychology

As our journey into the intricate universe of Artificial Intelligence (AI) progresses, we encounter the pivotal notion of Causal Inference. This cornerstone in the edifice of machine learning and its profound ties with human psychology and learning demand our attention. While the previous chapter dissected the importance and evolution of learning algorithms, this chapter aims to illuminate the role of causal inference within human cognition and AI frameworks.

Humans are innately equipped to recognize patterns and deduce causality. Our brains are expert architects of cause-effect relationships. Repeated sequences of actions and outcomes culminate in us inferring causal relationships. For example, touching a hot stove and subsequently experiencing pain leads us to promptly conclude that the heat is the cause. This instinctive ability to discern causality underpins human learning and decision-making.

The concept of causal inference, deeply woven into the fabric of psychology, influences our behaviors, beliefs, and worldview. It arms us with the ability to project future events, interpret past occurrences, and comprehend present situations. Our world perception and resultant actions are largely steered by our ability to infer causality, whether accurately or inaccurately.

In the realm of machine learning, causal inference emerges as a burgeoning discipline, holding the potential to catalyze significant advancements. Traditional algorithms primarily zero in on detecting correlations within data. But crucially, correlation does not imply causation. Causal inference, conversely, strives to unravel the cause-effect relationships interwoven between variables.

Models within machine learning that harness causal inference attempt to mirror human understanding of causality. They not only seek to identify patterns but also endeavor to decode the cause-effect relationships underpinning those patterns. This ability to deduce causal relationships endows these models with enhanced predictive accuracy, particularly when faced with distributional shift—a situation characterized by changes in data distribution.

The fusion of causal inference and AI heralds an exciting paradigm shift. As machines begin to grasp causality akin to humans, they transform from mere pattern detectors to cognitive entities capable of understanding and reasoning. This cognitive leap enables AI systems to offer justifications for their predictions and decisions, enhancing their transparency and reliability.

Furthermore, an understanding of causal relationships can augment AI's competence in world interaction. Within reinforcement learning, a subset of AI where an agent learns decision-making through environment interaction, causal inference can bolster the agent's decision-making prowess by comprehending the causal repercussions of its actions.

The integration of causal inference into AI architectures signifies a momentous stride towards the realization of Artificial General

Intelligence (AGI), a scenario where machines can comprehend, learn, and apply knowledge as effectively as a human.

As we shift our gaze to the ensuing chapter, we will delve into Bayesian Inference, another fundamental concept tethering AI and psychology. As we traverse this crucial terrain, we will expose the utilization of this statistical method within human cognition and machine learning, thereby continuing our exploration of the intricate interconnectedness binding AI, psychology, and learning.

Chapter 37: Bayesian Inference:
Bridging Human Cognition

With the rich landscape of causal inference behind us, our intellectual expedition now veers toward the intriguing terrain of Bayesian Inference. This chapter aims to delve into the intersection of Bayesian Inference with human cognition and AI. This fusion of seemingly disparate fields will shed light on the fascinating interplay between psychology, learning, and artificial intelligence.

Bayesian Inference, deeply entrenched in human cognition, fundamentally drives our daily decisions and learning. At its core, it is a statistical inference method enabling us to refine our beliefs about the world as we assimilate new evidence.

In human cognition, Bayesian inference represents the cognitive mechanism by which we recalibrate our subjective probabilities or beliefs in response to the newly acquired information. For example, if you entertain the possibility of rainfall today, observing dark clouds congregating in the sky would lead you to revise your belief, consequently increasing the likelihood of rain in your estimation.

The Bayesian model of cognition posits that our minds intuitively employ the principles of Bayesian statistics. This Bayesian framework offers a mathematical explanation of how evidence should be employed to revise beliefs, a process strikingly similar to the innate human approach to learning and information processing.

In AI, particularly machine learning, Bayesian Inference occupies a pivotal role. It provides a mathematical blueprint for machines to adjust their models or hypotheses based on observed data.

For instance, in a Bayesian machine learning model, the model's parameters are considered random variables with prior distributions. As fresh data is introduced, these distributions are updated, enabling the model to learn from the data. Like human learning, this updating process permits the model to enhance its predictive and decision-making abilities.

Furthermore, Bayesian methods provide a systematic approach to combat overfitting, a prevalent challenge in machine learning. Overfitting arises when a model excessively learns from the training data, resulting in subpar performance on unseen data. Bayesian methods resolve this issue by harmonizing the model's complexity with the volume of available data, thereby enhancing the model's ability to generalize to new data.

The marriage of Bayesian Inference and AI creates pathways for models that can learn from data in a manner reminiscent of human learning. Applying Bayesian methods enables AI to learn from experience more effectively, adapt to novel situations, and make robust decisions amidst uncertainty.

In addition, Bayesian methods imbue AI with transparency, providing a window into the learning process and the rationale behind predictions. Bayesian models mirror how humans intuitively comprehend and reason about the world by quantifying uncertainty and delivering probabilistic predictions.

Chapter 38: Decoding AI's Lexicon

Following our comprehensive examination of Bayesian Inference, our intellectual voyage now steers toward the captivating realm of lexicographic sorting algorithms. In this chapter, we shall unravel the complex layers of these algorithms and illuminate their fundamental role within AI systems' operations.

0000	abcd	abcd	abc	ab	a	∅
0001	abc	abc	abcd	abc	ab	a
0010	abd	abd	abd	abcd	abc	ab
0011	ab	ab	ab	abd	abcd	abc
0100	acd	acd	acd	ac	abd	abcd
0101	ac	ac	ac	acd	ac	abd
0110	ad	ad	ad	ad	acd	ac
0111	a	a	a	a	ad	acd
1000	bcd	bcd	bcd	bc	b	ad
1001	bc	bc	bc	bcd	bc	b
1010	bd	bd	bd	bd	bcd	bc
1011	b	b	b	b	bd	bcd
1100	cd	cd	cd	cd	c	bd
1101	c	c	c	c	cd	c
1110	d	d	d	d	d	cd
1111	∅	∅	∅	∅	∅	d

Lexicographic sorting, colloquially known as alphabetical or dictionary order, is a systematic method to arrange words or sequences of characters in a specific order. This system holds a prominent position in language-based processing systems, which include language translation, text analysis, and natural language understanding in AI. The term 'lexicographic' is borrowed from 'lexicography', the discipline of creating and revising dictionaries. In lexicographic sorting, the ordering of words or character strings mirrors that found in a dictionary, considering each character from left to right.

Various algorithms can execute lexicographic sorting, including quicksort, heapsort, and mergesort. These algorithms share a common foundational principle: they compare elements based on their relative position in the lexicographic sequence. To illustrate, suppose we wish to sort the words 'AI', 'Psychology', and 'Learning'. A lexicographic sorting algorithm would compare the initial character of each word. In case of a tie, the algorithm progresses to the subsequent character and continues until it encounters a difference or exhausts characters for comparison. The resulting sorted sequence would be 'AI', 'Learning', and 'Psychology'.

Lexicographic sorting finds a critical application within AI, particularly in Natural Language Processing (NLP), where it facilitates tasks such as information retrieval, language translation, and sentiment analysis. For example, search engines utilize lexicographic sorting to fetch and rank search results based on user-provided keywords. Similarly, in machine translation systems, lexicographic sorting aids in the dictionary lookup processes, mapping words in the source language to their equivalents in the target language.

When we examine the nexus of lexicographic sorting, learning, and psychology, intriguing parallels come into view. Human cognition employs a sorting variant when acquiring new vocabulary or understanding the syntax of a language. While this process is undoubtedly more intricate and nuanced than its algorithmic counterpart, it does share a systematic approach with lexicographic sorting algorithms. Further, studying and implementing lexicographic sorting algorithms can augment our understanding of AI and its cognitive processes. By scrutinizing these processes, we enhance our understanding of both human and artificial cognition and advance further toward decoding the complexities of learning.

Our exploration continues in the subsequent chapter, where we shift our attention toward the concept of Heuristic Search, another vital component in AI systems. We will delve into its underlying principles and scrutinize its role in decision-making processes in both human cognition and AI. In doing so, we will further decode the complex nexus of psychology, learning, and artificial intelligence, providing insights into the remarkable emergence of sophisticated systems from simple interactions.

Chapter 39: Consequential AI: A Societal Perspective

Artificial Intelligence (AI) stands on the precipice of a revolution, with advancements propelling it toward the ability to make significant, transformative decisions. As underscored by Dr. Ronald Baecker in his discourse, "What Society Must Require of AI," this revolution necessitates a deep dive into the core attributes that would foster societal trust in AI systems.

The AI landscape has undergone a substantial metamorphosis, moving away from its rudimentary beginnings. Now, with the advent of machine learning, AI can make consequential decisions, a realm historically the exclusive domain of humans. This development foregrounds a dichotomy between nonconsequential and consequential AI systems. While nonconsequential systems can afford occasional missteps, as they rarely make critical decisions, consequential systems tackle complex issues where mistakes could have severe implications.

These consequential AI systems, responsible for decision-making in autonomous vehicles, medical diagnoses, judicial decisions, and military drones, operate in spheres where errors could potentially result in the loss of human lives. The challenge lies in enhancing the accuracy of these systems and equipping them with decision-making abilities on par with human decision-makers, as suggested by Baecker.

However, a pair of critical questions presents itself: How can we detect a mistake made by an AI system, considering the complexity of machine learning processes? And how can we trust the outcomes, particularly when the system's decision-making process may be too convoluted to elucidate?

Consider an AI system deployed in a court of law to predict a defendant's likelihood of re-offense. If the system's decision-making process is shrouded in opacity, how can the defendant challenge the decision that could profoundly impact their liberty?

Building trust in consequential AI systems requires stringent standards. Baecker posits that these systems should emulate human decision-makers, displaying competence, dependability, transparency, trustworthiness, accountability, empathy, compassion, fairness, and justice. Furthermore, developing these systems should focus on effectively utilizing context, intuition, and discretion.

Baecker's views set high expectations for AI systems to be deemed trustworthy. Yet, for society to bestow upon them the responsibility of making life-altering decisions, these conditions must be satisfied. As the evolution of AI forges ahead, the focus should be on imbuing these traits into AI systems and fostering societal understanding of the necessity of these standards to mitigate unwarranted expectations or apprehensions.

Undoubtedly, the dawn of consequential AI signals a significant milestone in the narrative of emergence, underlining the increasing sophistication of AI due to a multitude of simple interactions. As we continue to navigate this evolving landscape, integrating these human-like qualities into AI systems will be a testament to our deepening understanding of AI and our own cognitive processes.

Chapter 40: Consequential Decision-Making in Artificial Intelligence

Artificial Intelligence (AI) has advanced from its humble beginnings of rule-based systems to intricate learning algorithms. It now holds a significant role in many sectors, from autonomous vehicles and healthcare to finance and law enforcement. Despite these advancements, most AI applications can still be classified as 'nonconsequential,' serving as supportive entities whose operations are monitored and decisions validated by human overseers.

The distinction between nonconsequential and consequential AI systems raises a compelling question: When does AI transition from offering mere assistance to exerting substantial, consequential influence over human lives? This chapter takes a deep dive into this defining 'tipping point' in the evolutionary trajectory of AI.

With continual advances in machine learning and big data, AI is on a steady march toward a critical threshold where it begins to execute consequential decisions independently. This transition implies AI systems gaining dominion over decision-making in critical realms, where errors could have substantial ramifications, such as in medical diagnoses or autonomous driving. These decisions not only directly impact the immediate stakeholders, but their influence reverberates across societal norms, ethics, and legal frameworks. The repercussions can be far-reaching and significant, marking this transition point as a distinctive milestone in our technological evolution.

Comprehending this transition entails an examination of various factors, technological and psychological alike. On one hand, it involves assessing technological capabilities, such as the power of machine learning and big data analytics. On the other hand, it necessitates understanding the psychological implications of entrusting consequential decision-making to AI systems.

As AI edges closer to this pivotal tipping point, society is presented with unique challenges. Among them are the need to establish trust and transparency in AI systems, the systems' potential impact on the job market and skills development, and the broader societal implications of their decisions.

But the question remains: How do we shape AI systems to undertake such consequential decisions responsibly and transparently? This task calls for more than technological innovation; it necessitates the establishment of robust legal and regulatory frameworks.

The evolution of AI, especially its transition towards consequential decision-making, reflects the emerging complexity of the interaction between technology and psychology. This evolution also underscores the compelling narrative of emergence, the ongoing process whereby complex systems and patterns arise from a multiplicity of relatively simple interactions. Thus, AI's journey to consequentiality doesn't just signal a shift in technological capabilities, it also encapsulates the very essence of the emergent phenomena that define our world.

Chapter 41: Illusions of Intelligence:
Perception of Sentience

Navigating the AI Landscape: The Emergence of Intelligent Chatbots

Artificial intelligence has become influential, leaving its mark in various sectors. This is a focal area where considerable progress has been made in chatbots. A pioneering leap has been achieved by developing AI-driven chatbots such as ChatGPT, which leverage machine learning algorithms and the breadth of natural language processing (NLP) to engage in dynamic and meaningful dialogues with users.

Chatbots have transitioned from basic rule-based systems with specific tasks to intricate AI entities with human-like characteristics. These entities are capable of deep learning and context-responsive interactions. This profound change stems from comprehensive research and technological advancements in NLP and machine learning, facilitating the creation of sophisticated algorithms and data-driven models that generate convincing dialogues.

The "Mirror Self-Recognition Test" (MSR), traditionally used in animal psychology to measure self-awareness, involves an animal's ability to recognize its reflection in a mirror. When applied to artificial intelligence, the sentient mirror test gauges an AI system's capacity to recognize and contextualize its state and interactions with the environment.

AI chatbots, such as ChatGPT, are not sentient in the traditional sense. They lack self-awareness or consciousness and do not pass the sentient mirror test because they do not comprehend the notion of self. However, they exhibit complex interactive behavior and responsiveness, creating an illusion of intelligence and sentience.

The sophisticated interplay of communication between humans and chatbots often leads to perceiving chatbots as sentient entities, a concept attributable to the Turing Test. Alan Turing suggested that if a machine's responses are indistinguishable from a human's, the machine can be deemed intelligent.

This mirrors how AI chatbots function. While they lack self-awareness, their capacity to generate human-like responses creates an illusion of consciousness, a phenomenon called pseudo-consciousness.

The evolution of AI chatbots provides insights into the direction of AI as it continues to explore new territories. While the intricacy of human consciousness is far from replicated in AI, the expanding capabilities of AI chatbots hint at a future where these systems might display increasingly sophisticated pseudo-consciousness, perpetually reshaping our understanding of intelligence and consciousness in artificial intelligence.

The narrative of AI is an ongoing saga, underscoring the human pursuit of knowledge and the human mind's capacity to innovate and create. Although AI chatbots like ChatGPT might not fully replicate human cognition's intricacy and richness, they serve as significant tools for further exploration and comprehension of cognitive science and artificial intelligence's interconnectedness.

Chapter 42: The Trolley Problem Revisited

In the scenario presented, we find ourselves entangled in an age-old philosophical conundrum, one which echoes the classical Trolley Problem but presents it in a novel and modern context. Here we see AI, charged with its directives and equipped with a deep understanding of situations and outcomes, faced with the dilemma of the bank robber philanthropist.

Let's examine the decision-making process of a hypothetical AI observer. Being armed with an in-depth understanding of the laws, the AI would clearly recognize the illegality of the robber's actions. But simultaneously, it would compute the positive outcomes resulting from these actions: the alleviation of suffering and the survival of a large number of orphans. This conflict, the clash of lawfulness and utilitarian outcomes, forms a formidable decision-making challenge for AI.

How might an AI, with its ability to compute vast amounts of data and predict future outcomes, address this dilemma? In a scenario like this, the AI would need to weigh various factors in its algorithmic process. These factors might include the probable future trajectories of the orphans, the potential punitive measures for the bank robber, and the societal impact of condoning or condemning the act.

We should also consider the precedent this decision may set. If AI opts to withhold information about the crime because it serves a greater good, it indirectly endorses utilitarian criminality. On the contrary, if it reports the crime, it prioritizes the sanctity of the law but risks endangering the welfare of the orphans.

This thought experiment exposes the difficulty of programming ethical decision-making within AI. It becomes increasingly complex as we move away from binary choices into the realm of moral ambiguity, where AI must weigh competing values against each other in intricate, real-world contexts.

Exploring these dilemmas doesn't provide us with definitive answers, but rather, highlights the potential challenges we face as we continue to intertwine AI into our lives, our societies, and our moral frameworks.

Chapter 43: Weighing Lives: Consequential Decisions of AI

The scenario you've described plunges us into the depths of what is known as the 'Trolley Problem,' a classic ethical conundrum that has provoked much debate. Its application in the context of autonomous vehicles and artificial intelligence is especially interesting and relevant.

In this scenario, the AI system of a self-driving car faces a choice: to continue on its path, striking and likely killing a diplomat who holds information crucial for preventing a global conflict, or swerve, sacrificing the two passengers to save the diplomat.

With current AI capabilities, predicting and valuing the potential contribution of an individual to future global events is well beyond their scope. It would require not just an understanding of that person's role and significance, but also a deep appreciation of geopolitical relationships, a predictive ability that currently eludes even the most sophisticated of human minds, let alone AI.

However, if we allow ourselves a hypothetical leap and imagine an AI system capable of making such a nuanced judgement, the scenario becomes an embodiment of a consequential ethical dilemma: is it acceptable to sacrifice a few to save many?

Various ethical frameworks provide different answers. Utilitarianism, for instance, would advocate for the decision that results in the greatest good for the greatest number, hence potentially justifying the sacrifice of the two passengers. In contrast, rights-based ethics could argue that the rights of the passengers not to be harmed should not be violated, regardless of the potential greater good.

The scenario underscores the complexity of designing AI systems to make consequential decisions. Without a universally agreed-upon ethical framework, how should we program AI to resolve these dilemmas?

Moreover, this scenario underlines the profound necessity for transparency in AI decision-making. If AI systems are to make decisions that could significantly impact human lives, the reasoning behind these decisions must be made clear. Otherwise, the acceptance of AI's consequential role in society may be hard to achieve.

Understanding the different ethical frameworks is essential for grappling with the complexities of decision-making in AI. These philosophies help guide actions and decisions based on different principles and values.

Utilitarianism, as mentioned earlier, is an ethical framework that prioritizes the greatest good for the greatest number. It's a form of consequentialism, with the rightness or wrongness of an action determined by its overall impact on welfare. For instance, an autonomous vehicle programmed with a utilitarian perspective would choose the action that minimizes overall harm, regardless of who is at risk.

However, Utilitarianism isn't the only perspective to consider. Deontological ethics, for instance, focuses on the inherent morality of actions, regardless of their outcomes. According to this philosophy, certain actions are right or wrong in themselves, regardless of their consequences. Applied to AI, a deontological perspective could argue that an autonomous vehicle should always follow traffic rules, even if breaking those rules could sometimes minimize harm.

Virtue ethics, another ethical theory, posits that the moral character of the acting agent is most important. Decisions should align with virtues such as honesty, kindness, and courage. In the context of AI, this might translate into programming systems to emulate certain 'virtuous' behaviors, such as fairness or transparency.

Lastly, we have rights-based ethics, which places the fundamental human rights of individuals at the forefront. This approach could argue that AI systems should always prioritize preserving human life and avoid actions that could harm individuals.

These are just a few examples of the numerous ethical frameworks that exist. Each provides a unique lens through which to examine the decisions made by AI systems, and each comes with its own set of strengths and weaknesses.

Chapter 44: Life and Death Decisions: The Psychologist's Role

In the arena of end-of-life care, the role of psychologists in interdisciplinary teams has gained prominence. They help individuals communicate better, understand their emotions, and make informed decisions, enhancing the prospect of dying with dignity. In the theatre of AI emergence, an analogous role for psychologists is envisioned, albeit in a different context.

Psychologists' understanding of human cognition, emotions, and decision-making patterns could be pivotal in developing AI systems capable of interacting more profoundly with humans. As AI systems grow more sophisticated, their capability to comprehend and respond to human emotions and motivations could be critical in healthcare settings, including end-of-life care. The use of AI in such sensitive scenarios needs careful and considerate design to preserve the dignity and individuality of the person involved.

For instance, let's consider an AI healthcare companion assisting a terminally ill patient. The AI must be calibrated to respond empathetically to the patient's emotional state, maintain respectful communication, and support them in making informed decisions about their care. Here, psychological theories could provide the necessary scaffolding to build these AI capabilities.

Yet, developing an AI system capable of such delicate human interaction presents considerable challenges. Not only technical hurdles but ethical considerations surrounding the deployment of AI in such situations must be addressed. Thus, psychologists, along with AI developers and ethicists, form a crucial component of the interdisciplinary teams tackling these issues.

The implications of psychologists' involvement in AI development extend beyond healthcare settings. As AI systems permeate various facets of human life, the need to understand and cater to human psychological needs increases. In the next chapter, "Embracing the Unknown: Preparing for the Unforeseen in AI Emergence," we explore how we can prepare for the unpredictable aspects of AI emergence.

Afterword

As we reach the closing pages of "Emergence II - An In-Depth Study of the Psychology of Artificial Intelligence," I find myself reflecting on the remarkable journey that led to the creation of this book.

First and foremost, I want to extend my heartfelt gratitude to Kevin and Marc. Our intellectual conversations not only served as a catalyst for this writing but continually challenged and inspired me. You both provided me with insights that transcended ordinary thought; I am eternally thankful for that.

I must also acknowledge the readers of my previous work, "Emergence-Dawn of a Conscious AI." Your curiosity, support, and thoughtful inquiries propelled me to delve deeper into this fascinating interplay between human psychology and artificial intelligence. This second installment stands as a testament to your engagement and encouragement.

My appreciation also goes to those in the AI and psychology communities, colleagues, researchers, and friends whose groundbreaking work continues to shape our understanding of these complex and intertwined disciplines.

Writing this book has been a profoundly enriching experience, allowing me to explore and articulate thoughts on a subject that resonates with our times and potentially our future. I sincerely hope that this work serves not just as a study but as a roadmap, a guide to handling the remarkable and sometimes daunting landscape of emergent AI systems.

Lastly, to you, the reader, thank you for embarking on this intellectual adventure with me. Whether you are a seasoned expert or a curious novice, I hope this book has provided insights, sparked your imagination, and challenged your understanding.

The future of artificial intelligence is a journey we all partake in, and I am honored to have shared a part of that path with you.

With deepest thanks,

Larry Lee Matthews is a visionary author and thought leader in artificial intelligence and psychology. With a keen interest in exploring the intricacies of human cognition and AI, he has dedicated his career to understanding the intersection of these disciplines.

Matthews's debut work, "Emergence-Dawn of a Conscious AI," captivated readers with its groundbreaking exploration of conscious artificial intelligence. His passion for unearthing deeper insights into AI's psychological aspects fueled the creation of "Emergence II - An In-Depth Study of the Psychology of Artificial Intelligence."

Known for his ability to simplify complex subjects, Matthews has provided a platform for readers to apply modern theory and psychological principles to AI's current and future applications. His writings offer insights into AI's rapid evolution's practical implications and potential challenges.

www.ingramcontent.com/pod-product-compliance
Lightning Source LLC
Chambersburg PA
CBHW071004050326
40689CB00014B/3482